Flight Briefing for Pilots

Volume 1

By the same authors

Flight Briefing for Pilots, Volume 2
(An Advanced Manual of Flying Training
complete with Air Instruction)

Flight Briefing for Pilots, Volume 3
(Radio Aids to Air Navigation)

Flight Briefing for Pilots, Volume 4
(Associated Ground Subjects)

A Guide to Aircraft Ownership

The Tiger Moth Story

Captains and Kings

Flight Emergency Procedures for Pilots

Check Pilot

Flying the VOR

Radio Navigation for Pilots

The Instrument Rating (N. H. Birch)

Flight Briefing for Pilots

Volume 1

An introductory manual of flying training complete with air instruction

N. H. Birch MSc, MRAeS
Director Hamilton Birch Ltd.
Liveryman of the Guild of Air Pilots and Air Navigators

and A. E. Bramson MRAeS
Chairman of the Panel of Examiners
Liveryman of the Guild of Air Pilots and Air Navigators

Illustrated by A. E. Bramson

FOURTH EDITION

PITMAN

PITMAN PUBLISHING LIMITED
39 Parker Street, London WC2B 5PB

Associated Companies
Copp Clark Limited, Toronto
Pitman Publishing New Zealand Ltd, Wellington
Pitman Publishing Pty Ltd, Melbourne

© N. H. Birch and A. E. Bramson 1978

First published in Great Britain 1961
Reprinted 1963, 1965, 1966, 1967, 1968
Second Edition 1970
Reprinted 1971, 1972, 1973
Third Edition 1974
Reprinted 1976, 1977
Fourth Edition 1978

ISBN: 0 273 01164 2

Text set in 10/11½ pt VIP Times, printed by photolithography and bound in
Great Britain at The Pitman Press, Bath

Preface

The value of formal pilot training geared to a proper syllabus was probably first demonstrated in 1916 when Lt. Smith-Barry was recalled from the Western Front during World War I and given a free hand to run No. 1 Reserve Squadron, Gosport. Here he put into operation his then very advanced ideas on flying training.

Since that time most of the Air Forces of the world have developed their flying training using the 'Gosport System' as a basis. However, although many countries produce excellent flying training manuals for their service pilots, often the civil trainee has had to make do with little more than typed notes.

At most of the smaller flying schools the main burden of training occurs during weekends and it is a long-established fact that there is a tendency on the part of hard-pressed flying instructors to take their pupils on an air exercise before ground instruction of any kind has been given. Time and again such a practice has proved to be thoroughly bad from every point of view. It was to fill the need for a simple manual of flying training that the authors wrote Volume 1 of the *Flight Briefing for Pilots* series. The book is strictly a pilot handling manual; everything possible has been done to ensure simplicity and all background information has been confined to essentials. Those looking for complicated mathematical formulae should seek this in the various excellent books written for aerodynamicists and aircraft designers – other than a few simple graphs in the appendix this work is essentially practical in its approach to the subject.

The purpose of this book (and the advanced Volume 2) is twofold. It gives the student pilot an easy-to-read explanation of how and why an aircraft flies before outlining the various exercises needed to gain a Pilot's Licence. Its second function is to provide a flight practice section for each air exercise. While this step-by-step handling sequence is useful reading for the pupil its main value is to provide the flying instructor with a basis for his air instruction or, to use the correct term, 'patter'; this has to be synchronised with the various demonstrations in the air. Consequently Volumes 1 and 2 should prove a valuable work of reference to those studying for a Flying Instructor's Rating. The syllabus and flying sequences conform to those approved by the UK Civil Aviation Authority.

Wherever possible the authors have tried to conform with the training techniques recommended by the UK Panel of Examiners, a body appointed by the Civil Aviation Authority and responsible for the testing of civil flying instructors in Britain. At the same time they would like to express their very real appreciation for the help and advice they have received from the Royal Air Force Central Flying School and individual members of the Panel of Examiners who have, from time to time, offered valued advice.

When Volume 1 first appeared the publishers and the authors hoped it would enjoy sufficient acceptance to encourage the production of additional volumes. Volume 2, which deals with the advanced exercises, was in due course followed by Volume 3 (Radio Aids to Air Navigation) and Volume 4 (Associated Ground Subjects). By 1977 the number of volumes in use had reached a total of 200,000 copies and since many of these have found a home many miles from their native land the authors have produced this completely revised edition which, it is hoped, will be more suited to international needs.

NHB
AEB

NOTE

The numbers in heavy type at the bottom of all pages dealing with the flying sequences conform to the British Flying Training Syllabus.

Australian, Canadian and South African student pilots will find it useful to relate these to their own syllabuses on pages viii and ix.

Contents

	Preface	v
	Table of Air Exercises	viii
	Introduction – Fundamentals of Flight	1
1	Familiarization with Aircraft	20
2	Preparation for Flight and Action after Flight	25
3	Air Experience	31
4	Effects of Controls	33
5	Taxying	45
6	Straight and Level Flight	51
7	Climbing	58
8	Descending	62
9	Turning	74
10	Stalling	92
11	Spinning	101
12	Take-off and Circuit to Downwind Position	106
13	The Circuit, Approach and Landing	124
14	First Solo	144
15	Advanced Turning	146
16	Operation at Minimum Level	153
17	Forced Landings:	
	a) without Power	164
	b) with Power	171
18	Pilot Navigation	185
19	Instrument Appreciation	215
	Appendix 1 – Graphs	224
	Appendix 2 – Ground Signals	228

Table of Air Exercises

| AUSTRALIAN SYLLABUS | | CANADIAN SYLLABUS | |
Exercise	UK Exercise	Exercise	UK Exercise
1 Aeroplane Familiarization	1	1 Familiarization	3
2 Preparation for Flight	2	2 Aircraft Familiarization and Preparation for Flight	2
3 Taxying	5	3 Ancillary Controls	4
4 Operation of Controls	4	4 Taxying	5
5 Straight and Level Flight	6	5 Attitudes and Movements	4
6 Climbing	7	6 Straight and Level Flight	6
7 Descending	8	7 Climbing	7
8 Turning	9	8 Descending	8
9 Stalling	10	9 Turns	9
10 Sideslipping	included in 8	10 Flight for Range and Endurance	6
11 Take-off	12	11 Slow Flight	6
12 Approach and Landing	13	12 Stalls	10
13 Spins and Spirals	11, 15	13 Incipient Spins and Full Spins	11
14 Emergency and Special Procedures (a) Engine failure (i) partial (ii) complete	17a	14 Spiral Dives	15
		15 Sideslipping	8
(b) Precautionary search and landing (c) Action in event of fire (i) engine fire (ii) other causes	17b 1E	16 Take-off	12
		17 The Circuit	12, 13
(d) Ditching	17	18 Landing	13
15 Instrument Flying Navigation	*19 18	19 The First Solo	14
		20 Illusions Created by Drift/Low Flying	16
		21 Off Airport Approach Procedures	17a
		22 Forced Approaches and Landings	17b
		23 Pilot Navigation	18
		24 Instrument Flying	*19
		25 Night Flying	Ex. 20, Volume 2

*Appreciation only. Fully explained in Volume 2.

*Appreciation only. Fully explained in Volume 2.

SOUTH AFRICAN SYLLABUS

Exercise		UK Exercise
1	Cockpit Layout	1
2	Preparation for Flight	2
3	Air Experience	3
4	Effects of Controls	4
5	Taxying	5
6	Straight and Level Flight	6
7	Climbing	7
8	Descending	8
9	Stalling	10
10	Medium Rate Turns	9
11a	Descending Turns	9
11b	Climbing Turns	9
12	Take-off (including engine failure during and after take-off)	12
13	Approach and Landing (including going round again)	13
14	Spinning	11
15	First Solo	14
16	Sideslipping	included in 8
17	Steep Turns	15
18	Instrument Flying	*19
19	Low Flying	16
20	Crosswind Landing and Take-off	12, 13
21	Precautionary Landings	17a
22	Forced Landings	17b
23	Action in the Event of Fire	1E
24	(reserved)	
25	Aerobatics	Volume 2
26	Night Flying	Volume 2
27	Navigation	18

*Appreciation only. Fully explained in Volume 2.

Flight Briefing for Pilots, Volume 2 contains the advanced exercises which are outside the requirements of a UK Private Pilot's Licence in its basic form. These are:

5	Taxying (Twin-engined)
19	Instrument Flying
20	Night Flying
21	Aerobatics
22	Formation Flying
23	Multi-engine Conversion

Introduction

Fundamentals of Flight

Since the beginning of time, Man has cast envious eyes on the birds of the air, but it is only within living memory that powered flight has been possible, the emergence of the petrol engine making his ambitions a reality.

For many years before the Wright Brothers made the first powered flight in 1903, a considerable fund of aerodynamic data was being amassed in various countries, notably by Otto Lilienthal experimenting with his gliders in Germany. To many about to take up flying, the fascinating principles which make flight possible are as great a source of mystery as they were to the pioneers of a century ago.

These notes are written with a view to explaining, without entering into mathematics, why an aeroplane flies. Obviously in the course of such an explanation simplicity must not be achieved at the expense of accuracy.

'As Light as Air'

The phrase 'as light as air' is a common one, yet air has weight. Imagine a cubic foot of air. If it were possible to place it on a pair of accurate balances in a vacuum it would weigh in the region of $1\frac{1}{3}$ oz. Indeed the air in an average-size room would weigh 130 lb and a large hall may contain several hundred-weight. Were it not for this fact an aeroplane would be incapable of flight.

A small piece of metal weighing $1\frac{1}{3}$ oz can be supported without effort on the palm of a hand; yet fired from a gun it will penetrate three or four feet of timber. What has happened to the piece of metal to give it such power? Its rapid movement has given it **Momentum** which, provided the movement is fast enough, will exert tremendous force. When moved at speed the $1\frac{1}{3}$ oz cubic foot of air will also gain momentum and it too will generate a force on meeting an object, the power of the force being dependent upon the speed of airflow and the shape of the object.

It is this force which, when coerced in the right directions by the aircraft designer, makes it possible for the aeroplane to fly, be it a light plane or a 150-ton transport aircraft.

Airflow Effect

The unexpected happens to air (or for that matter any fluid such as water) when it is made to flow around objects of a certain shape.

An interesting experiment with two sheets of stiff notepaper bent across the middle will illustrate this. By holding the two pieces as shown in Fig. 1 with their creases approximately one inch apart they can be made to close together by blowing hard between them.

In effect the impossible would seem to have happened. The

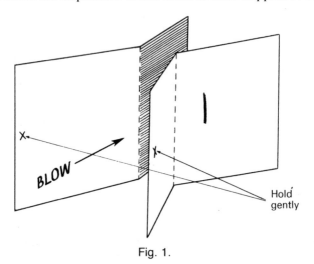

Fig. 1.

explanation is as follows: the air is forced through a passage which progressively becomes narrower. In order to pass through the restriction it must increase its speed (Fig. 2). A law of nature demands that when a moving fluid is forced through a restriction in this way, the increase in speed is accompanied by a drop in pressure. It is this drop in pressure which causes the sheets of paper to close together.

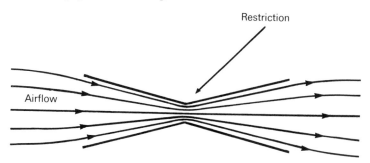

Fig. 2. The airflow as it passes between the two sheets of paper.

A similar experiment can be made with a large tablespoon. If this is held downwards and brought into contact with a running tap, the water will pull the spoon into the jet instead of pushing it away (Fig. 3). Here again the fluid (in this case water) is made to flow around the contours of the spoon, causing a decrease in pressure.

A shape almost identical to the back of a spoon is incorporated in the wing of an aeroplane and a section cut through its width would reveal a remarkable similarity.

The shape which is shown in Fig. 4 is called an **Airfoil Section** and it is the basis upon which flight depends.

Behaviour of an Airfoil Section

By introducing smoke into a jet of air flowing over a model wing, it is possible to watch the behaviour of the stream which is forced over the top surface and that which passes below (Fig. 5).

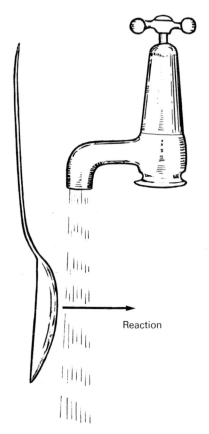

Fig. 3. When held in a jet of water the back of a spoon reacts in a similar manner to the bent paper in Fig. 1.

The previous paragraph explained that a drop in pressure occurs on the top surface, but if the **Leading Edge** of the airfoil is raised at a slight angle to the airflow, because of its momentum, pressure will rise when the air makes contact with the undersurface of the wing (Fig. 6).

The net result is that the airfoil section will generate a lifting force approximately two-thirds of which results from the

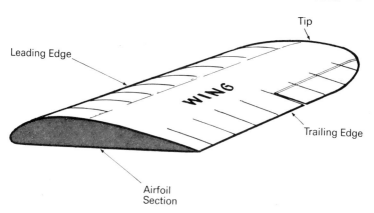

Fig. 4. A wing showing the airfoil section.

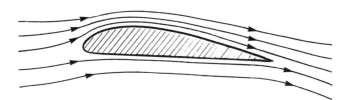

Fig. 5. The flow of air around the airfoil section.

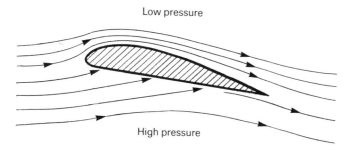

Fig. 6. The build-up in pressure under the airfoil which adds to the force caused by the decrease in pressure on top.

decrease in pressure on top of the wing and one-third from the increased pressure below. **Lift,** as the force is called, can be increased by making the air flow faster. It can also be controlled in another way, by altering the **Angle of Attack.**

The angle of attack is the angle between the airfoil and the airflow relative to it (Fig. 7).

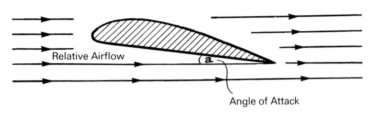

Relative Airflow

Angle of Attack

Fig. 7. The angle of attack.

It should be emphasized that the angle is between the *relative* airflow and the airfoil so that the same angle of attack could occur under differing flight conditions such as climb, straight and level flight, or gliding (Fig. 8).

Lift is generated from most parts of the airfoil and if it is measured and represented pictorially the distribution of force would be as shown in Fig. 9. It is more convenient to depict these individual forces in one line drawn at the point from which the total effect occurs. This point is know as the **Centre of Pressure** (Fig. 10).

Assuming a steady airflow of say 100 kt, if the angle of attack is increased then the amount of lift increases. At the same time the centre of pressure moves forward – the significance of this will be explained later.

Unfortunately while producing lift the airfoil also creates a less desirable force known as **Drag.** Clearly any body in a moving fluid such as air must cause resistance and while the lift acts at right angles to the relative airflow, drag will of course be parallel to it (Fig. 11).

The functions of lift, drag and the centre of pressure should now be considered under various angles of attack. In the

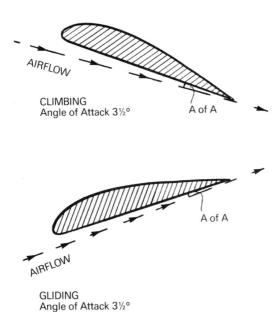

CLIMBING
Angle of Attack 3½°

A of A

A of A

AIRFLOW

GLIDING
Angle of Attack 3½°

Fig. 8. The relative airflow.

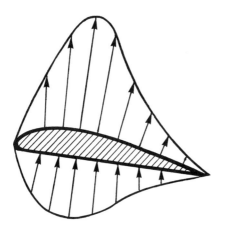

Fig. 9. The distribution of pressure around an airfoil.

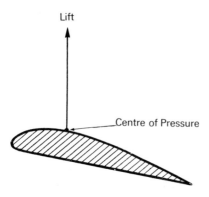

Fig. 10. The lift force acts from the centre of pressure.

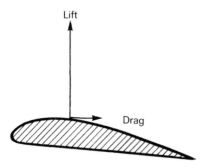

Fig. 11. The drag force acts at 90° to lift.

diagrams which follow it can be seen that, as the angle of attack increases, the lift force becomes more powerful and the centre of pressure moves forward. At the same time drag increases, slowly at first up to approximately 4° but more rapidly as the angle increases. The greatest amount of lift for the least amount of drag or **Best Lift/Drag Ratio** as it is called usually occurs at $3\frac{1}{2}°$–4° (Fig. 12).

A point is reached when further increases of angle will produce no more lift. Taking the extreme case, if the wing were to be forced through the air at 90° angle of attack there would

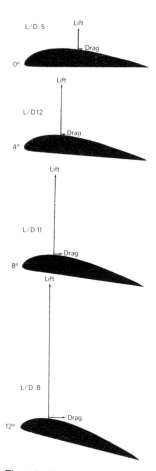

Fig. 12. The effect of angle of attack on lift and drag.
These forces, as depicted by the length of the arrows, are shown to scale; the figures on the left refer to the lift/drag ratio for a typical airfoil.

be no lift at all, only a considerable amount of drag. At some point between 0° and 90° marked deterioration occurs. This is known as the **Stalling Angle** and it will be dealt with more fully in Chapter 10. Graphs showing lift and drag with changes of angle of attack are in Appendix 1.

There are other factors which affect the amount of lift a wing can generate and these are given in the following summary—

1   *Angle of Attack.* At a given airspeed an increase in angle up to the stalling angle gives more lift.

2   *Airspeed.* For a given angle of attack the faster the airspeed the more lift for a particular wing.

3   *Airfoil section.* There are many variations of these shapes each designed for a purpose (Fig. 13). By and large, the deep,

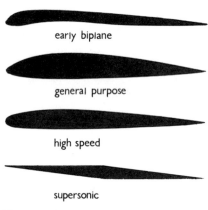

early biplane

general purpose

high speed

supersonic

Fig. 13. Some typical airfoil sections.

highly cambered airfoils give the most lift for a given speed while thinner sections are used when a high cruising speed is required of the design.

4   *Wing area.* The larger the area of wing of a given airfoil section the more weight it will support at any particular speed.

5   *Air density.* The weight of air varies with height and temperature, being little more than half as dense at 20,000 ft as it is at sea level. The more dense the air the more lift a particular wing will give for a particular airspeed.

Creating the Airflow

For the purpose of explanation the airfoil has been assumed to be stationary with an airflow moving over it. In practice this is not the case. Bearing in mind that it is the *relative airflow* which provides lift it will be realized that, by moving the wing through the air at speed, lift and drag will occur in exactly the same way. In a helicopter this is arranged by having two or more wings rotate around a central point with a linkage to control the angle of attack. In an aeroplane the relative airflow is generated by pulling (or pushing) the entire machine through the air.

Forward motion achieved by driving the wheels like a car would terminate as soon as the aircraft lifted off the ground. Instead the engine rotates an **Airscrew** (popularly known as the Propeller). Explained in simple terms airscrew describes its function well, since it does in fact move itself through the air like a large wood screw. It would be a more accurate, however, to consider each **Propeller Blade** as a wing since they are of airfoil section and so provide lift in a horizontal plane. It is this force which thrusts the aeroplane through the air; indeed, the force which causes the aeroplane to move forward is called **Thrust.**

The propeller may be rotated by a piston engine or a **Gas Turbine (Turbo-propeller).** Alternatively a **Turbojet** can be employed to produce thrust direct without the use of a propeller. In this case thrust is the reaction to the considerable mass of air ejected from the rear of the engine.

The Aeroplane

The parts of the aircraft explained in the preceding pages may now be assembled.

First, there is the wing of airfoil section. In order to generate lift, a means of propelling it through the air must be attached, in this example a petrol engine driving an airscrew (Fig. 14).

This strange assembly is incapable of controllable flight because it lacks a characteristic which is of prime importance to any vehicle whether motor-car, boat or aeroplane—**Stability**. Taking a simple case the term can be applied to a handcart. With the greatest of difficulty it would be possible to balance the vehicle illustrated in Fig. 15, but the slightest tilt would become more and more pronounced, with disastrous results.

Fig. 14. The wing with a means of propulsion added.

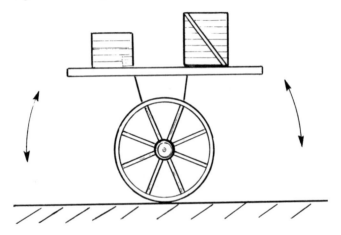

Fig. 15. An unstable vehicle.

The wing of airfoil section is equally unstable. Referring back to the behaviour of the centre of pressure, it will quickly be realized that for this strange craft to remain in balance its centre of gravity must coincide with the centre of pressure.

Imagine the aeroplane is flying with its lift and weight in balance as shown in Fig. 16 when a disturbance in the air lifts the front of the machine slightly, thus increasing the angle of attack. The immediate effect on the centre of pressure has already been made clear: it will move forward.

If the two lines of force marked lift and weight in Fig. 17 are imagined to be lengths of string pulling in the direction of the

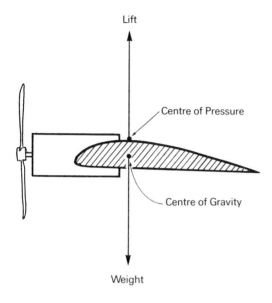

Lift

Centre of Pressure

Centre of Gravity

Weight

Fig. 16. Balanced on a knife edge.
The arrangement is as unstable as the vehicle in Fig. 15.

arrows, it can be seen that by moving forward, the centre of pressure has added to the nose-up disturbance.

The two forces now produce a 'nose up' motion which still further increases the angle of attack. This in turn causes the centre of pressure to move forward again and the machine will commence a series of uncontrollable rotations.

The remedy is simple. In the case of the handcart, shafts are incorporated as in Fig. 18. Part of the function of the 'driver' is to stabilize the handcart through these shafts. A remarkably similar arrangement is used by the aircraft designer. To the wing is attached the **Fuselage:** this not only acts as the shaft of the handcart but also houses the engine, pilot and passengers and in many cases other items such as fuel and freight. In place of the man at the end of the shaft is a small surface called the **Tailplane.** Its function is to stabilize the behaviour of the

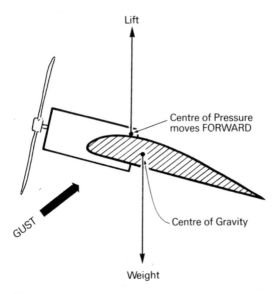

Fig. 17. The centre of pressure has moved forward and upset the balance.

Mainplane (wing). In America the tailplane is referred to as the Stabilizer.

It is the tailplane which gives the aircraft **Longitudinal Stability.** Usually the tailplane is of a symmetrical airfoil section giving no lift when at 0° angle of attack. Should a disturbance cause the nose to rise, the tailplane assumes a positive angle and produces lift which, acting through the leverage of the fuselage, will bring the mainplane back to its original position. In the event of a gust causing the nose of the aircraft to drop, the tailplane will assume a negative angle of attack and produce a corrective force in a downward direction. Reference to Fig. 20 will make the function of the tailplane clear.

Notwithstanding the addition of a fuselage and tailplane the machine would still be unstable **Directionally,** i.e. it would tend to wander from left to right. **Directional Stability** is attained by fixing a vertical surface, similar to half a tailplane, on top of the rear fuselage. This is called the **Fin** and its function is very

Fig. 18. A simple cure for an unstable vehicle.

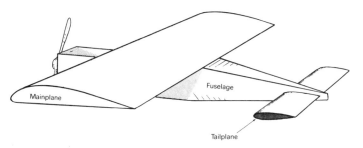

Fig. 19. The addition of a fuselage and tailplane.
This cures the instability illustrated in Figs. 15, 16 and 17.

similar to that of the tailplane except that it operates in the directional sense. Fig. 21 shows that the fin is assisted in its function by the sides of the fuselage which are of greater area behind the centre of gravity of the machine than in front. Complete with fin the assembly is akin to a weathercock in its action.

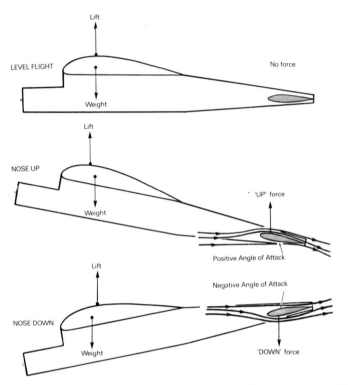

Fig. 20. In level flight there is no lift from the tailplane because of its symmetrical airfoil section.
A 'nose-up' or 'nose-down' movement causes the tailplane to generate lift in a correcting sense.

Fig. 21. The 'keel area' and the fin give the aeroplane directional stability.

Lastly the aeroplane must remain level and not roll from side to side. To achieve this **Lateral Stability** as it is called, the designer has several alternative methods at his disposal. By placing the wing on top of the fuselage as shown in Fig. 22 (i.e. **High Wing Monoplane**) and keeping the centre of gravity low, the machine will behave like a pendulum. Indeed such a method is known as **Pendulous Stability.** It should be understood that the lift comes off the wings at right angles as shown in Fig. 22,

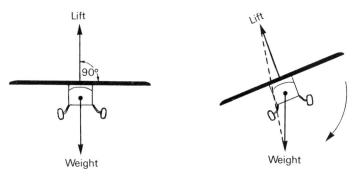

Fig. 22. One of several methods used for lateral stability: a high wing causing pendulum action.

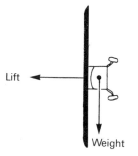

Fig. 23. Aeroplane in a 90° bank attitude.
Under these circumstances the aeroplane cannot maintain height.

whereas weight always acts vertically downwards. In the extreme case of an aeroplane on its side, none of the lift from the wings would oppose weight and height could not be maintained.

Not all aeroplanes are high wing monoplanes and other methods of attaining lateral stability are successfully employed, a common one being to incline each wing upwards at a small angle to the horizontal so that when the aircraft is level the tips are above the centre of the wing where it meets the fuselage. This is called **Dihedral** and the angle between the horizontal and the wing is the dihedral angle. In explaining how dihedral improves lateral stability it is necessary to anticipate Fig. 29 which shows that a bank on its own causes an aeroplane to sideslip towards the lower wing (fully explained in Exercise 4). Because of the dihedral angle, during a sideslip the relative airflow will meet the lower wing at a larger angle of attack than the raised wing, thus increasing lift on the dropped wing and raising it in the process. In a perfectly straight wing the angle of attack is constant along its span during a sideslip and at least 3° dihedral is needed to improve lateral stability. Some high wing monoplanes have dihedral to assist pendulous stability. Stability is discussed in greater detail in Volume 2.

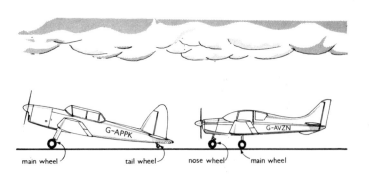

Fig. 24. The two most common types of undercarriage.
Sometimes the nosewheel or tailwheel is steerable through the rudder bar.

The aeroplane must have something on which to manoeuvre during taxying, take-off and landing and the **Undercarriage** which performs this function may be fixed or, in the interest of reducing drag, **Rectractable.** It may be of **Tailwheel** or **Tricycle** design (Fig. 24). Each type has its own advantages and disadvantages.

In addition the designer must attempt to reduce drag by **Streamlining** all items such as wing bracing struts, undercarriage legs, windscreen, engine cowlings, etc.

It only remains to explain how the aeroplane is made to climb, glide, turn, etc. These manoeuvres are accomplished by the **Controls** and their management is the subject of the following pages.

1 Familiarization with the Aircraft

The aim of this exercise is to acquaint the student with the function and position of all controls in the aircraft.

Before the student is able to assimilate flying instruction it is imperative that he should be fully conversant with the position of the controls and instruments. Some aircraft are equipped with a **Basic 'T' Flight Panel** of instruments set in a standard layout in relation to one another. Such a full panel will enable the student to fly in cloud at a later stage in his flying training. Alternatively there may be a **Limited Panel** consisting of essential instruments only. Some aircraft are confined to the simplest flying controls while others include such items as flaps, variable pitch propellers and retractable undercarriages.

The fuel system must be fully understood and when more than one tank is involved the management of the relevant fuel cock(s) is of utmost importance. Operation of the brakes will be explained by the instructor who will also describe the electric system and its **Master Switch.** It is standard practice to fit two separate ignition systems on aeroplane engines and each is controlled either by a separate tumbler switch or a multi-position ignition key. When no electric starter is fitted it is necessary to turn the engine by hand and a special magneto is often installed which generates a spark at low speeds. The switch controlling this magneto must be known before starting is attempted.

The student will be acquainted with the location of the First Aid kit and the fire extinguisher and its method of operation.

Before starting, taking-off, stalling/spinning, landing etc. certain checks of the aircraft's systems and controls must be made. These may be conducted from memory using easy-to-remember mnemonics, or, alternatively, check lists can be used. While a check list is invariably used in the multi-crew operation of complex aircraft, it can prove a trap for the single-crew pilot unless he is careful to ensure that ALL items are read off the list and carefully checked. Never do a check partly from memory and partly with the aid of a check list. That is the way to forget important items.

These notes are of necessity written in broad terms and the student pilot is well advised to learn all he can about the aircraft which is to be his classroom. Full details will be found in the Owners/Flight/Operating Manual published for the aircraft type.

Emergency Exercise 1E: Action in the Event of Fire

The aim of this exercise is to teach the student the correct procedure to adopt in the event of an aircraft fire on the ground or in the air.

Fire in a modern aircraft is today an unusual occurrence, high standards of engineering and component efficiency making the risk of fire even more remote than the possibility of engine failure. Nevertheless, however unlikely its occurrence may be, fire on the ground or in the air should be looked upon as a form of lifeboat drill which is an essential part of the pilot's training. The pilot must understand the function and disposition of whatever fire appliances are installed in the aircraft.

Broadly speaking fires may be considered under two headings –

1 Those which occur in the cabin or fuselage.
2 Engine fires.

Cabin or fuselage fires may be caused by electrical faults. Since fuel vapour associated with the engine priming system may be present in the cockpit, under no circumstances should smoking be permitted unless the aircraft type allows.

Under normal circumstances the origin of cabin fires may be traced by the type of smoke or fumes, electrical faults usually **1E** producing a smell of burning rubber of insulating material whereas battery shorting gives off an acrid smell. After detection by the occupants, electrical faults may be pinpointed by the smoke, and then isolated with the relevant switch although usually the circuit fuse will have 'blown' as soon as the fault develops. When the main circuit is at fault the battery can be isolated by putting the **Ground/Flight** switch into the 'ground' position or alternatively when the battery is isolated by a **Master Switch** this must be turned off.

Non-electrical fires in the fuselage can be handled with the cabin fire extinguisher which should be removed from its bracket and directed by hand.

Fires in the engine may be caused by faulty induction or exhaust systems, over-priming during starting, and fuel or oil leakages under pressure. Larger aircraft are equipped with a fire-warning system in conjunction with a spray ring which is arranged to discharge over all vulnerable parts of the engine. In light aircraft the cabin fire extinguisher is sometimes arranged so that when it is operated in its bracket the discharge carries through a pipe into the engine induction manifold.

All engines are separated from the airframe by a fireproof bulkhead which prevents the engine fire from spreading to the cabin, fuselage or wings.

On the ground the minor fire caused by over-priming before starting already mentioned can be put out by smothering the flames with a chock, or folded tarpaulin, which should be held against the air intake.

In the air more serious fires caused by oil or petrol pipe fracture are complicated by the fact that while the engine is turning it will continue to pump petrol and oil. In the case of a petrol fire, turn off the petrol whether on the ground or in the air. In this way the carburettor, fuel pumps and exhaust system will be cleared of petrol and only when the engine stops running should the ignition be switched off. Usually it is best to glide ahead and contain the flames behind the fire wall, but when the need arises a sideslip will keep flames away from vulnerable areas. The cabin heater vent must be closed to exclude fumes.

1E   An oil fire can be recognized by the associated smoke. While the action of turning off the fuel will eventually stop a petrol fire in the engine, an oil fire may continue so long as the propeller rotates the engine causing it to pump oil under pressure. In the case of an oil fire, rotation should be stopped by switching off the ignition and holding up the nose so that the airflow is insufficient to turn the engine.

It will be appreciated that an engine fire can be quite minor, in which case the foregoing procedure would quickly bring it under control. When the fire extinguisher is discharged into the air intake the engine will breathe in the contents of the extinguisher and a major overhaul will be necessary before the engine can be used again. Therefore the extinguisher should only be used as a last resort when the fire persists.

Never attempt to re-start an engine which has caught fire in the air.

Note. Exercise 1E should only be practised when accompanied by a flying instructor and then at a safe height and within gliding distance of an aerodrome.

Flight Practice

COCKPIT CHECKS

a)   Trim for level flight.
b)   No insecure items in the aircraft.
c)   Carburettor heat control as required.

OUTSIDE CHECKS

a)   Altitude: sufficient for the manoeuvre and recovery.
b)   Location: not over towns, other aircraft or airfields or in controlled airspace.
c)   Position: within gliding distance of an aerodrome.

AIR EXERCISE

(For the purpose of this demonstration imagine a fire has occurred in the engine while in flight.)

1E

a) Throttle **Closed.**
b) Petrol **Off.**
c) Close the cabin heater vent.
d) Wait for the engine to stop running under its own power then turn the ignition **Off.**
e) If an oil fire is suspected stop the engine rotating by holding up the nose of the aircraft and reducing airspeed (simulate).
f) If necessary sideslip the flames and/or smoke away from the cockpit.
g) Should the fire persist operate the extinguisher.

2 Preparation for Flight and Action after Flight

The aim of this exercise is to acquaint the student with the correct methods of preparing for flight, engine starting and testing, and his responsibilities after flight.

Before any flight is commenced clearance must be obtained from Air Traffic Control. The details of a training flight are entered in the Flight Authorization Book and in the case of a student or any pilot undertaking a solo flight he will sign in the appropriate place indicating that he understands the details of the exercise his instructor requires him to practise.

It is the pilot's responsibility to check that the aircraft is serviceable and fuelled, by reference to the Record of Serviceability and/or by confirmation with the instructor or engineer in charge. He must also ensure that the aircraft is not overloaded and that it is within its centre of gravity limits (see Airfield Performance, Weight and Balance, Chapter 3, Volume 4).

Before boarding the aircraft the pilot must inspect it externally (**External Checks**), commencing by checking that the aircraft is suitably positioned with chocks in front of the wheels. The ignition switches must be in the 'off' position and when applicable it is good practice to remove the ignition key as a double check. The fire extinguisher must be safely stowed and its pressure must be indicating correctly. Also do ensure that there is a First Aid kit in the aircraft. Standard practice is to commence the external aircraft checks at the point of entry since the inspection will finish at this point, when the pilot can then enter the aircraft after a systematic check. Particular points for attention are listed in the aircraft manual, and will include freedom of the structure from damage, cracks and corrosion. Additionally the security of cowlings, hatches, fuel and oil filler caps should be checked. Oil and fuel contents should always be checked visually.

When an aircraft has been standing overnight there is a risk of condensation within the fuel tanks, when moisture from the air above the fuel will collect at the bottom of the tank in the form of water. This is most likely to occur when the tanks are only partly filled. The risk is obvious – water in the carburettor may stop the engine. To safeguard the carburettor and fuel lines from water and sediment contamination **Fuel Strainers** are fitted to the tanks and the lowest part of the fuel system. These must be drained into a glass or clear plastic jar before the first flight of the day, and the fuel inspected for water. Since fuel is coloured (green or blue) clear water will appear colourless. The strainers should be operated *before* re-fuelling has mixed the contents of the tank and dispersed the water within the petrol. Having operated the fuel strainers, be sure that they are properly closed before entering the aircraft, otherwise the tank will lose its contents through the strainer instead of supplying the engine. Tyres should be inspected for obvious loss of pressure and possibly **Creep.** Creep is the movement of the tyre in relation to the wheel and marks are painted on both which will be out of line when creep has occurred, with possible damage to the valve. The pitot covers (and when applicable to the aircraft type, static vent plug) and control locks should be removed and stowed in the correct place.

Some aircraft have a stall warning device which is operated by a small vane on the leading edge of the wing. The device may be tested on the ground after first switching on the battery master switch.

The condition of the propeller must be inspected and it should then be turned several times by hand before the first flight of the day. This is particularly important under cold conditions, assisting starting and providing an opportunity to check cylinder compressions. In the case of a radial or inverted engine this precaution will obviate the possibility of damage from hydraulic locking caused by oil or petrol drainage into the inverted cylinders.

When the generator or alternator is belt-driven its tension and condition should be checked while at the front of the aircraft.

After entering the aircraft the pilot should ensure that he will be comfortable in flight and adjustments to the rudder pedals, safety harness, seat position and/or the number of seat cushions, etc., should be made. This is of paramount importance.

The pre-starting **Internal Checks** are commenced by moving all controls to ensure full and free operation. When the rudder pedals are connected to the nose or tailwheel this check may have to be delayed until the aircraft is moving. The instruments should be examined for any obvious signs of unserviceability, e.g. broken glass, altimeter which will not set correctly, etc.

Unless it is possible to use an external battery, all unnecessary load (radio, rotating anti-collision beacon, etc.) should be switched off before starting so enabling the aircraft accumulator to provide the high current needed to turn the engine.

Starting the Engine

Most aircraft today are equipped with electric starters and the procedure for starting, which depends upon the type of installation, is laid down in the handling notes for the aircraft type. However there are still light aircraft without mechanical starting and these must be turned by hand. This is known as **Swinging the Propeller** or **Hand Starting.**

The procedure to be adopted in these cases is as follows—

(*a*) Ensure that the aircraft is sited on firm ground with the tail pointing away from other aircraft or open windows. Chocks should be in place and the brakes applied.

(*b*) Check the flying controls for full and free movement, and by visual reference determine that they move in the correct sense, i.e. stick to left – left aileron up and right one down; stick to right – right aileron up and left one down. Stick back – elevators up; stick forward – elevators down. Right rudder – rudder to right; left rudder – rudder to left.

Check the instruments for serviceability.

(*c*) Turn on the fuel and, with the mixture control in the 'fully rich' position, the engine should be primed either by the pilot or the starter (ground crew) when the type entails external priming. **2** (*d*) Call out to the starter '*brakes on: switches off: petrol on: throttle closed*' and check each item as it is said. The starter will repeat these items to the pilot and when ready will request '*throttle set: contact*'.

(*e*) Set the throttle to the starting position and switch on the **Impulse** magneto (specially designed for starting the engine), give the 'thumbs up' sign and repeat, '*throttle set: contact*'. The starter will then turn the engine over until it fires. Unless the propeller has stopped in a position difficult for the ground crew to reach, the switch must not be turned off between swings so avoiding the possibility of misunderstanding. To prevent nosing over, the stick should be held back on tailwheel types.

(*f*) When the engine starts turn the second magneto 'on' and check the oil pressure as it builds up to normal. If there is no indication of oil pressure, switch off immediately.

(*g*) Adjust the throttle so that the engine idles at 1,000 RPM (or fast enough to ensure operation of the generator) thus allowing it to warm up to working temperature.

(*h*) The engine may fail to start if it is too 'rich' when the starter will request '*switches off: throttle open*'. These instructions should be repeated and executed by the pilot who will give the 'thumbs down' sign when the starter will turn the engine in the opposite direction to normal thus blowing out some of the mixture. The starting procedure then continues from (*e*) after the starter has requested, '*throttle set: contact*'.

Cockpit Check (after starting)

(*a*) Check both switches are on (according to type).

(*b*) Check the anti-collision/strobe lights are on.

(*c*) Check the instruments as they apply to the particular aircraft (temperatures, pressures, and gyros erecting).

(*d*) When applicable check the engine-driven generator and also the operation of any radio equipment in the aircraft.

Testing the Engine

Note. When an oil temperature gauge is fitted see this is at the correct minimum temperature before attempting to 'run-up'.

Alternatively allow a warm-up period of five minutes for a cold engine.

(a) Change onto another tank to prove the fuel system.

(b) At 800–1,000 RPM check each magneto in turn by switching off and then on, thus determining that both are functioning at low engine speed.

(c) On tailwheel aircraft hold the stick right back and open the throttle smoothly and fully, at the same time checking the oil pressure. Check the RPM at full throttle, which should be within the limits for the type of aircraft, and without delay reduce power.

(d) At 1,600 RPM check each magneto in turn noting the decrease in RPM which must not exceed 100 at that speed. (RPM and permitted drop may vary from one aircraft type to another.) Apply carburettor heat and check for a small drop in engine speed.

(e) Check all temperatures and pressures along with vacuum supply for the instruments and electric charge.

(f) Now close the throttle against its stop and check the slow running.

Note. The full throttle test in (c) is usually only done before the aircraft's first flight of the day.

Running-down Procedure

(a) After flight allow the engine to idle at 800–1,000 RPM for half a minute or so thus allowing it to cool at an even rate. Uneven and rapid cooling may damage the engine.

(b) Check each magneto at idling speed and when ready to stop the engine operate the **Idle Cut Off.**

(c) After the engine has stopped, check—
   1. Switches off.
   2. Petrol off.
   3. Throttle closed.
   4. All radio and rotating beacon switched off.
   5. Gyro instruments 'caged'.
   6. Master switch 'off'.

2

Parking, Security and Picketing

When hangerage is not available the aircraft must be parked in a sheltered position and the following action taken:

(*a*) Ignition/Master Switch/Fuel off and mixture control in idle cut-off.

(*b*) Parking brake on.

(*c*) Pitot cover on.

(*d*) Control locks in position or, when none are fitted, the controls must be secured with the seat harness.

(*e*) When applicable (e.g. in strong sunlight) the canopy covers should be fitted.

(*f*) When strong winds are expected the aircraft must be tied down to picket or concrete blocks using the lashing points provided on the aircraft.

After Flight

When the detail has been completed the Authorization sheet should be signed in the appropriate column. Any defects in the aircraft or its equipment should be reported and entered in the 'snag book' kept at most flying schools.

3 Air Experience

The aim of this exercise is to familiarise the student with what may be a new sensation, flight in a light aircraft, and to make him aware of ground and other features likely to be seen.

The eagerly awaited first flight is intended to give the pupil pilot a little time to become accustomed to the sensation of flying before serious instruction begins. To those without previous flying experience the apparent lack of speed often creates something of an anti-climax which rapidly gives way to the sheer pleasure of seeing the countryside from above.

During this first flight local landmarks and their relationship to the aerodrome will be indicated by the flying instructor. While no serious attempt to teach is made on this first occasion, later in the flight the student will be invited to place his hands and feet lightly on the controls so that the remarkably small movements needed to produce a change in flight attitude are appreciated.

Throughout this book such phrases as 'move the stick' or 'push the stick' occur. In fact during most flight conditions these movements are in the nature of pressures rather than deliberate movements and to establish the necessary touch and appreciation of feel when flying a light aircraft the method of holding the control column is important. The stick should be held by the thumb and first two fingers only and not gripped in the fist, although this procedure may be necessary on heavy aircraft.

Study the instruments at intervals during the flight and determine the height of the aircraft (altimeter), the speed through the air (air speed indicator), and the RPM of the engine (engine speed indicator).

Above all relax and endeavour to become part of the aircraft, **3** allowing the body to go with the bank during a turn, rather than attempting to lean away from it. The importance of keeping a constant lookout cannot be overstressed. Some pupils tend to allow their attention to become devoted to the cockpit with the attendant risk of collision with another aircraft or even simply becoming lost through not maintaining a lookout. At an early stage in training the pupil should become accustomed to using the 'clock code' for reporting the position of other aircraft, straight ahead being 12 o'clock, 90° left nine o'clock, slightly to the right one o'clock, etc. The words 'high' or 'low' may be included in the report to describe an aircraft above or below. During later flights the instructor will expect his pupil to find his own way back to the airfield and as a homing aid the student should develop the habit of relating the sun to a part of the aircraft.

On this first flight, comfort and the ability to reach the controls with ease should be checked. Visibility out of the aircraft may need attention and, unless the seat is adjustable, cushions behind and beneath may be needed. An ideal arrangement should be found and adhered to when flying a particular aircraft.

4 Effects of Controls

The aim of this exercise is to teach the student the effect of the control surfaces, individually and interrelated, and also the effect of the supplementary controls.

The three principal controls are the **Elevators, Ailerons** and **Rudder.** Their position on the aircraft is illustrated in Fig. 25.

The elevators are actuated by backward and forward movement of the control column and they control the aircraft in the **Pitching Plane** (nose up/nose down during level flight). As

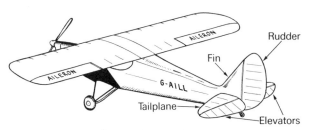

Fig. 25. The position of the control surfaces.

the aircraft pitches up and down so the angle of attack is altered, thus increasing or decreasing drag. Because of this the elevators also control the airspeed of the aircraft. This is shown in Fig. 26.

The ailerons are actuated by sideways movement of the stick and they control the aircraft in the **Rolling Plane** (left or right wing up or down). These movements are shown in Fig. 27.

The rudder is moved by the **Rudder Bar** and it controls the aircraft in the **Yawing Plane** (nose to left or right wing tip). **4**

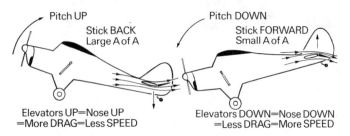

Fig. 26. The elevators are controlled by the backward and forward movement of the stick.

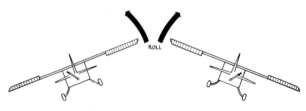

Stick to left=left aileron up & right down Stick to right=right aileron up & left down
=left wing down =right wing down

Fig. 27. The ailerons respond to sideways movement of the stick. The diagrams represent the rear view of their operation.

These movements are illustrated in Fig. 28.

To provide the desired effect on the aircraft, the elevators, ailerons and rudder are dependent upon the airflow over them and it therefore follows that they will be more effective at high speed than low. Furthermore in most single-engined aeroplanes the rudder and elevators are situated within the **Slipstream** from the propeller and for this reason are more effective with the power on than for instance during a glide, when the engine is throttled back. The ailerons being outside the slipstream are under the influence of the airflow only; therefore on many aircraft their 'feel' and effectiveness provide a good indication of airspeed.

In practice the movements of the stick are easily remembered. In whichever direction the stick is moved that part of the

4

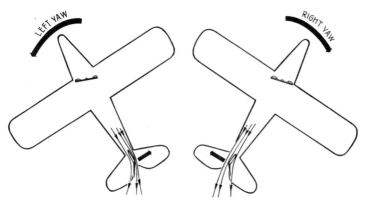

Left rudder pedal forward
=left rudder
=left yaw

Right rudder pedal forward
=right rudder
=right yaw

Fig. 28. The rudder bar activates the rudder.

aircraft will depress relative to the pilot, e.g. stick to left—left wing down; stick forward—nose down, etc. The movements and effects so far outlined are known as the **Primary Effects of Controls.**

The primary effects of rudder and aileron create additional or **Further Effects of Controls.**

Further Effects of Ailerons

If the stick is moved to the left the aircraft will bank to the left. Reference to Fig. 29 will show that the lift and weight forces are now out of line, thus causing the aeroplane to sideslip towards the lower wing which in this case is the left one. During this slip the side of the fuselage together with the fin and rudder will be subjected to the air flowing up to meet the aircraft as indicated in Fig. 30. Since the area affected is far greater behind the centre of gravity than in front the aeroplane will behave like a large weathercock, the nose turning towards the left wing *although the rudder is held in the central position.* Similarly if the **4**

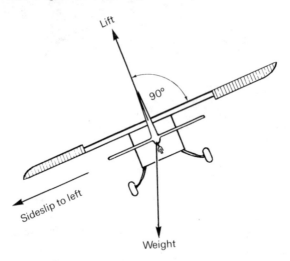

Fig. 29. Further effects of ailerons.
When the wings are banked, lift and weight are no longer in line and a slip towards the lower wing will result.

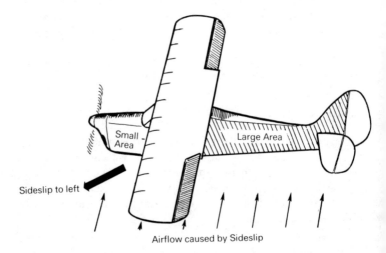

Fig. 30. The sideways component of the airflow is shown here causing a turn although the rudder is central.

4

stick is moved to the right, the right wing will go down and the nose will swing towards the lower (right) wing. If left to develop, a spiral dive to the left or right will result as the nose follows the lower wing down below the horizon.

Further Effects of Rudder

If the left rudder pedal is pressed forward the nose of the aircraft will swing towards the left wing tip. The outer (right) wing will move faster than the inner one (similarly the outer man in a wheeling column of troops steps long while the inner man marks time). Because of the faster airflow, the right wing in this case will produce more lift than the left and a bank will occur *although the control column is held in the central position* (Fig. 31).

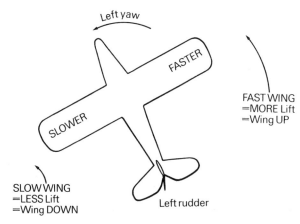

Left yaw

FASTER

SLOWER

FAST WING
=MORE Lift
=Wing UP

SLOW WING
=LESS Lift
=Wing DOWN

Left rudder

Fig. 31. During the yaw the inner wing is always slower than the outer which moves on a larger radius.

In the same way right rudder will produce a yaw to the right followed by a bank to the right. Because the nose follows the lower wing down below the horizon, a spiral dive to the left or right will develop.

From the foregoing it can clearly be seen that the ailerons and

4

rudder are closely related, and that the further effect of aileron is yaw and the further effect of rudder is roll.

The Trimming Controls

The purpose of these secondary controls is to take the load off the primary ones during the various conditions of flight. For example, having to hold back the stick during a prolonged climb or maintain forward pressure to obtain a desired airspeed in level flight would be tiring for the pilot.

The simplest form of elevator trim control consists of a small lever which is connected to the control linkage via a pair of tension springs. This arrangement is illustrated in Fig. 32 and

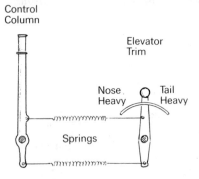

Fig. 32. The spring-loaded trim control used on old designs.

movement of the trim control alters the tension of the springs which apply pressure on the control column in the desired sense. Such a system is fitted to the vintage Tiger Moth and more recent designs e.g. the Piper Tomahawk. The most common method incorporates a small movable surface known as a **Trim Tab** which is mounted on the elevator and adjusted by the **Elevator Trim Control.** The airflow over this trim tab holds the elevator in the desired position without any effort from the pilot. Such a system can be seen on most aircraft (Fig. 33).

4   In normal conditions of flight the aircraft is in balance, but

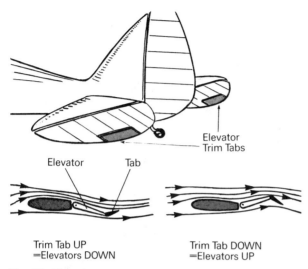

Elevator
Trim Tabs

Elevator   Tab

Trim Tab UP
=Elevators DOWN

Trim Tab DOWN
=Elevators UP

Fig. 33. The trim tab.

this can be upset by changes in weight distribution such as amount of fuel, number of passenger seats occupied, luggage, etc., carried. Changes of throttle will also upset this balance in direction, due to the twisting motion of the slipstream, and cause pitching, due to changes in thrust. Alterations in airspeed also upset the balance of the aeroplane since these involve changes in angle of attack with the attendant movement of the centre of pressure. All of these out-of-balance forces must be countered by the controls and the trimmer relieves the pilot who would otherwise be called upon to provide constant pressure on the stick.

Not all aircraft have a fixed tailplane and separate elevator of the type so far described, many modern designs featuring an **All Flying Tailplane** (Fig. 34). Originally developed for high speed aircraft where large out-of-balance forces must be catered for this type of control incorporates an **Anti-balance** or **Anti-servo Tab,** so linked that it moves in the same direction as the main control, its purpose being to prevent 'runaway control', e.g. the tendency for the stick to continue coming back after the pilot **4**

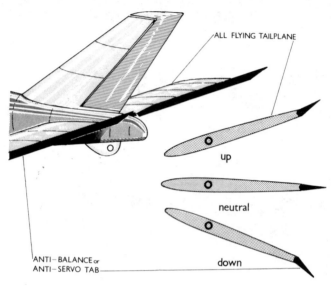

ALL FLYING TAILPLANE

up

neutral

ANTI–BALANCE or
ANTI–SERVO TAB

down

Fig. 34. All-flying tailplane
Note that the anti-servo tab is arranged to add control load as the
main surface is moved away from the neutral position

has applied backward pressure. The tendency for All Flying
Tailplanes to over-control is due to unstable movement of the
centre of pressure relative to the hinge point. This type of tab
should not be confused with the **Balance Tab** fitted to some
conventional elevators and other control surfaces for the purpose of assisting the pilot. These relieve the force required of
the pilot by moving in the *opposite* direction to the main control
(balance tabs are explained in greater detail on page 18 of
Volume 2 in this series). In many cases the datum setting of
balance or anti-balance tabs is adjustable from the cockpit via
the elevator trim control so enabling the tab to provide fore-
and-aft trim in addition to its other function.

While most light aircraft are fitted with an elevator trimmer
only, larger types have a rudder and in some cases aileron
trimmer also. Provided smooth conditions exist, a correctly
trimmed aircraft will fly 'hands off' in a climb, glide or level

flight.

Flight Practice

Cockpit Checks

a)   Set cruising power.
b)   Trim for level flight.

Outside Checks

a)   Altitude: sufficient for manoeuvre.
b)   Location: not over aerodromes or towns or in controlled airspace.
c)   Position: check in relation to a known landmark.

Air Exercise

Primary Effects of Controls

a)   Move the stick to the left and the left wing goes down. Centralize control and level the wings.
   Repeat to the right and notice instrument indications.
b)   Press the stick gently forward and the nose falls away and goes below the horizon. Notice airspeed increasing and a loss of height. Move the stick back and the nose comes towards the cockpit and above the horizon. Check instrument indications and note airspeed decreasing and a gain in height.
c)   The elevator movements are the same irrespective of the attitude of the aircraft. Now bank gently to the right and move the stick back and then forward. The aircraft's pitching behaviour will be the same in relation to the pilot.
d)   From straight and level flight move the left foot forward on the rudder pedals and notice the nose swings towards the left wing tip. At the same time a skid to the right will be felt and this will be indicated on the **Slip Indicator.**
   Repeat to the right.
e)   Now bank gently to the left and apply right rudder. The nose will swing up towards the high (right) wing and left rudder will cause the nose to yaw towards the left wing and go below the horizon. In other words the rudder produces the same movement irrespective of the attitude of the aircraft.
f)   Notice that control effect is proportional to control movement.

4

Further Effects of Controls

a)   *Rudder.* Hold the stick in the central position and apply left rudder. The nose will swing towards the left wing tip and a roll will commence to the left developing into a spiral dive in the same direction.

Resume straight and level flight and repeat to the right.

b)   *Ailerons.* With the rudder in the central position move the stick to the right. A bank to the right will result followed by a yaw towards the right wing tip which will continue into a spiral dive in that direction.

Revert to straight and level flight and repeat to the left.

Effect of Airspeed and Slipstream

a)   At a high power setting, climb at 70 kt* and notice how sensitive are the elevators and rudder. Also note the feel of the ailerons.

b)   Now close the throttle and glide at 70 kt. The elevators and rudder will be less sensitive and a larger movement will be required to produce the same effect as before (with slipstream). The ailerons will feel the same.

c)   Now fly at a low airspeed and note the feel of the ailerons. Increase to maximum speed and the ailerons will become heavier and more sensitive giving a good indication of airspeed.

Effect of Power

a)   In cruising flight trim the aircraft and remove the hands and feet from the controls.

b)   Open the throttle and very soon the nose will rise and the aircraft climb. At the same time a turn will develop in the opposite direction to propeller rotation. Rudder and forward elevator pressure are required to maintain balanced level flight.

c)   Return to cruising flight then close the throttle slightly. The nose will drop, a loss in height will occur and a turn will develop in the same direction as propeller rotation. Rudder and back pressure on the elevators are required to keep the aircraft in balanced level flight.

Effect of Trim

a)   From straight and level flight move the trim control to a 'nose heavy' position. Notice that backward pressure on the stick is required

*Use speed appropriate to type of aircraft.

to maintain the same airspeed. Should the stick be allowed to ride in the 'hands off' position the nose will drop and speed will increase.
b)   Repeat this procedure moving the trimmer to a 'tail heavy' position when a forward pressure will be required to maintain the original airspeed. When left to fly 'hands off' the nose will rise and the airspeed will decrease.

Effect of Flaps

a)   Reduce speed until the IAS is within the flap limiting range (white arc). Re-trim and notice the attitude of the nose relative to the horizon.
b)   Lower 10 degrees of flap and notice the change in trim. Maintain the same airspeed and compare the new nose position. It is lower in relation to the horizon. The aircraft is now descending and more power is required to maintain height. Notice the improved response of the rudder and elevators.
c)   Lower full flap and note the change in trim and reduction in airspeed. Trim the aircraft to hold approach speed.
d)   Now raise the flaps and feel the considerable change in trim as a result.
e)   Whenever the flap position is altered there will be a change in nose attitude and trim.

Operating the Mixture Control

a)   At a safe height set cruising power.
b)   Slowly bring back the mixture control until there is a slight drop in RPM (further leaning of the mixture will cause rough running and eventually a position is reached when the engine will stop).
c)   During cross-country flights the best fuel economy for any particular power setting will be obtained by moving back the mixture control until the RPM decrease, then easing it forward to the point where the RPM are just restored to the original setting.

Operating the Carburettor Heat

a)   Note the RPM, then operate the carburettor heat control. Notice the drop in RPM.
b)   When carburettor ice is present (denoted by a decrease in RPM and eventual rough running) use of the heat control will first cause a further drop and, when the icing is severe, more pronounced rough-

4

ness before the RPM increase. At this stage the carburettor heat control should be returned to cold when the RPM should have returned to the previously set engine speed.

c)   Do not use part heat since under certain weather conditions this could raise the temperature into the icing range and cause carburettor icing.

Cabin Heat and Ventilation

a)   Note the position of the heat and cabin air controls. (Some aircraft allow heat to be directed to the windscreen.)

b)   Apply heat and notice that it may be controlled according to the needs of the occupants.

c)   When applying heat it is good practice to open a fresh air vent as a guard against possible fumes.

d)   Should ice form on the windscreen in flight, direct all heat to the windscreen using the control provided.

e)   If necessary open the clear vision panel (when fitted).

5 Taxying

The aim of this exercise is to teach safe control of the aircraft on the ground, and the brake, full rudder and instrument function checks.

An aircraft is controlled and manoeuvred on the ground by the use of power, rudder and brakes, either independently or interrelated.

During taxying the flaps must be raised to avoid damage by flying stones, etc.

Most aircraft of modern design have tricycle undercarriages, direction on the ground being maintained via the nose wheel which is usually linked to the rudder pedals.

Aircraft should always be taxied slowly and never in a straight line unless the pilot can see directly ahead as in the case of an aircraft fitted with a nose wheel. Normally with tailwheel undercarriage forward vision is restricted by the nose-high ground attitude and to maintain a satisfactory lookout he must turn the aircraft from side to side. Speed should always be kept low to give the pilot adequate time to see, think and manoeuvre the aircraft.

Use of Power

Surface type determines the amount of power required for taxying. For example, on grass more power is required to propel the aircraft than on concrete. When moving off from a standstill in order to overcome the inertia of the aircraft, considerable power may be needed. Once the aircraft is moving, power is reduced and the student should aim to select a power setting that will keep the aircraft moving at a constant safe speed, normally a fast walking pace.

Under certain circumstances it may be necessary to increase the amount of power, for example during turns, or while taxying up an incline. On tailwheel aircraft slipstream will increase the effectiveness of the rudder although when taxying in a strong crosswind braking assistance may be necessary in addition to the slipstream effect.

Speed is controlled by adjusting the throttle setting (power) but when fully closing the throttle fails to slow the aircraft brake must be applied.

Turning

The aircraft may be turned by use of rudder alone, or in the case of aircraft with tailwheels or castering nosewheels, rudder assisted by increasing its effect with slipstream, and/or braking. Care should be taken not to make sudden changes of direction except at very low speed since the turn may 'build up' resulting in a swing which can be difficult to control. Normally additional thrust is required to overcome the friction caused by braking and care should be taken not to lock one wheel (particularly when moving forward from rest) since turns on a locked wheel cause stresses on the undercarriage, distortion of the tyre and possibly tyre creep with the attendant risk of a damaged valve.

On aircraft with tailwheels fairly coarse use of rudder is often needed to produce a turn, particularly in a crosswind.

Use of Brakes

On first moving off from the parked position the throttle must be closed and the brakes tested immediately. They should always be used carefully, particularly when flying tailwheel types, since harsh application may cause the aircraft to nose over, damaging the propeller. They should be applied gently and the amount of braking should be progressively reduced as the aircraft slows down. Prolonged braking should be avoided, especially when the assistance of the brakes is required to maintain direction in a strong crosswind. Excessive braking may heat up the brake drum with adverse effect on the tyre and

5

tube, resulting in reduced tyre life and brake effectiveness. Disc brakes are fitted to most modern trainers and other light aircraft and these are considerably less prone to 'fading' than drum brakes. When a tail skid is the only brake (vintage aircraft), ample room must be allowed when stopping.

Use of Flying Controls (Tailwheel types)

Normally the controls should be in the neutral position, but the stick must be held back when traversing soft grass or rough ground. The effect of slipstream over the elevators ensures that the tail remains firmly on the ground and counteracts any tendency to nose over. The trimmer may be used to assist the backward pressure on the stick. When taxying downwind the stick should be held forward to prevent the wind acting under the tail surfaces and lifting the rear of the aircraft.

The Effect of Wind (Tailwheel types)

Taxying into wind or downwind presents no problem. However, the effect of a crosswind blowing on the side or keel surface tends to weathercock the aircraft into the wind. In light or moderate crosswinds use of rudder assisted by the slipstream is usually adequate to maintain direction. In strong crosswinds taxying becomes more difficult and additional assistance from the brakes may be required. To avoid prolonged braking it may be possible to 'tack' and this method is preferable to extended use of the brake.

The Tricycle Undercarriage

Aircraft with this type of undercarriage are much simpler to taxi than tailwheel designs, having better directional stability on the ground and providing for the pilot an unobstructed view ahead. The student pilot must nevertheless resist the temptation to taxi fast or make excessive demands of the brakes.

5

Instrument Checks

At a later stage in his training the student pilot may progress to instrument flying and learn, among other exercises, how to enter low cloud on instruments after take-off. Clearly such an exercise places reliance upon the mechanical function of the instruments at a crtical phase of the flight so that before take-off the pilot must take steps to ensure that these are functioning correctly. It is therefore essential that the student should develop the habit of checking the correct operation of his instruments while taxying. The procedure is explained under 'Ground Practice'.

Rudder Function Check

While many aircraft have a fully castering nosewheel and others incorporate a nosewheel linked to the rudder control by springs, a number of designs feature a direct linkage between the rudder pedals and the nosewheel steering. In these aircraft it is only possible to check for full and free rudder movement while taxying. This check must be done at a low speed.

Ground Practice

Control of Speed

(*a*) Unscrew the throttle friction nut to obtain ease of movement. Ensure that all is clear ahead, increase the power until the aircraft has moved forward a few feet, close the throttle and apply the brakes to check that they are functioning correctly.

(*b*) Increase the power and move forward; reduce power to maintain a constant safe speed which should be controlled with throttle. Reduce power when running downhill and add power when taxying uphill. Use power and brake to control speed according to surface.

5

Control of Direction

(*c*) Select a point on which to maintain direction and apply rudder to move the aircraft from side to side to obtain satisfactory forward visibility. Maintain a good lookout all around. (On tailwheel aircraft note the effectiveness of the rudder with and without slipstream. Swing the nose from side to side to improve the view ahead.)

(*d*) Use the brakes very carefully at first getting the feel of them and noting their effect when applied with rudder to make a turn or together to stop the aircraft. Avoid using the brakes in opposition to power.

(*e*) When turning apply rudder in the desired direction if necessary assisted with brake. Apply more power if needed to keep the aeroplane moving. Make sure you are clear to turn then, at a low speed, apply full rudder (left and right) to check for full and free movement.

Instrument Check

(*f*) Check the function of the instruments (according to equipment). Turn right and the Compass and the Direction Indicator will increase in heading, the turn needle shows a turn to the right and the balance indicator shows a skid to the left. Now repeat these checks while turning to the left. During the turns the Artificial Horizon should remain level, only responding when the aircraft tilts or rocks while taxying. The Vertical Speed Indicator should indicate no gain or loss of height and on a level airfield the Altimeter should indicate the height shown before taxying commenced.

Emergencies Ex. 5E

Should the brakes fail while taxying –

    (*a*) Close the throttle.

    (*b*) Turn away from obstacles and allow the aircraft to roll to a halt.

5E

(*c*) If necessary increase rolling friction by turning onto the grass.

(*d*) If the aircraft continues to roll and a danger of collision exists operate the idle cut-off, turn off the fuel and switch off the ignition and master switch.

6 Straight and Level Flight

The aim of this exercise is to teach the student to fly at a constant speed, height and direction.

When an aircraft is flying at a constant speed, height and direction the forces acting on it are in equilibrium, i.e. lift equals weight and thrust equals drag (Fig. 35). A change in any one of

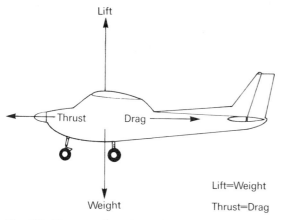

Lift=Weight

Thrust=Drag

Fig. 35. The aeroplane in straight and level flight is in a state of equilibrium.

these forces will bring about a change in the others. For example, if power is increased, the thrust will be greater than the drag and the aircraft will accelerate. The increase in speed will produce an increase in lift and since the lift component will now be greater than the weight, the aircraft will begin to climb. Conversely, when power is reduced, thrust becomes less than drag and the aircraft will slow down until thrust and drag are in balance. The lower speed will reduce lift and the aircraft will descend.

Changes in throttle setting have an effect on the directional stability of the aircraft in addition to altering the amount of thrust. The tendency to yaw when the power setting is changed results from **Slipstream Effect.** This is illustrated in Fig. 36 and

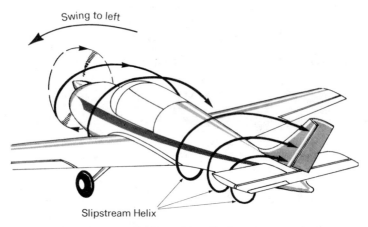

Fig. 36. The slipstream helix and its effect on the aeroplane.

it should be explained that, influenced by the rotation of the propeller, the slipstream travels back around the fuselage in a helical path. Able to pass freely under the rear fuselage, the helical slipstream makes contact with one side of the fin and rudder, thus deflecting the tail of the aircraft to one side and causing a swing. The direction of swing will depend upon the rotation of the engine, most modern power plants turning in a clockwise direction when viewed from behind.

To overcome slipstream effect, the designers may use one or more of the following methods –

(*a*) Arrange a spring (sometimes adjustable in flight) to hold on rudder in the desired direction.

(*b*) Attach a small metal tab to the trailing edge of the rudder.

6

This is set on the ground by bending in the direction necessary to hold on rudder.

(c) Offset the fin at a slight angle in order to give a permanent force in the opposite direction to the swing.

(d) Install the engine out of line with the fuselage so that the airscrew pulls to one side and counteracts the swing.

(e) Fit an adjustable trim tab to the rudder.

Unfortunately, with the exception of (d) and (e) and the adjustable version of (a), all of these arrangements only work perfectly at cruising speed, the condition for which they are set, and changes of throttle upset the balance of the system. A rudder trim, which can be adjusted from the cockpit is of course the best arrangement.

Good straight and level flying is the basis of cross-country flying and the ability to fly in a straight line at a pre-determined height and airspeed will take the student pilot some time to master. Exercise 4 has explained fully the inter-relation between rudder and aileron. While large deviations from heading usually require the use of both controls, small corrections can be made on the ailerons alone.

Hunting the Airspeed is a common fault. As the term implies the student pilot will go from 'too slow' to 'too fast' in a series of prolonged pitching movements. This is caused by not allowing the airspeed to settle before making any corrections. Over-correction and incorrect use of the trim control are perhaps the commonest faults of all.

For any condition of flight it is correct practice to think in terms of attitude in relation to the horizon and the position for cruising speed should be learned. Once the aircraft has settled, small corrections to the speed are made by raising or lowering the nose. In other words the airspeed is always controlled by the elevators (angle of attack) and the purpose of the throttle is to determine whether the aeroplane will gain height, maintain height or descend at any particular airspeed. Small height corrections may be made with the elevators, trading speed for height.

Obviously, if the speed is increased above normal cruising, **6** more power will be needed to maintain height. On the other hand a reduction of speed by moving the stick back will cause the aeroplane to climb unless the power is decreased, and the method of adjustment is outlined under flight practice.

The aeroplane differs from other vehicles in a manner which is perhaps unique. There is a speed which requires the smallest possible amount of engine power for level flight. If an attempt is made to reduce this speed by holding up the nose the aeroplane will begin to sink and *more* power will be required to maintain height. Indeed, because of the very rapid increase in drag which is experienced at high angles of attack (and high drag requires high thrust to balance the forces), the lowest possible flying speed requires *full* throttle. At the other end of the scale, maximum speed also demands full power in order to balance the high drag resulting from the faster airflow (see graph 3, page 226).

Flight Practice

OUTSIDE CHECKS

a)   Altitude: sufficient for manoeuvre.
b)   Location: not over aerodromes or towns or in controlled airspace.
c)   Position: check in relation to a known landmark.

AIR EXERCISE

Attaining the Level Attitude

a)   At the required altitude place the nose of the aeroplane on the horizon in the approximate straight and level attitude.
b)   Hold the aeroplane in this position and as the required speed is approached set the throttle to cruising RPM.
c)   Allow the speed to settle and move the elevator trimmer until no pressure is required on the stick. Make any adjustments to the airspeed which may be necessary by adjusting the attitude with the stick and re-trim.
d)   With the airspeed correct check the height. If the aeroplane tends

6

to climb reduce the power slightly and lower the nose a little. On the other hand a gradual loss of height indicates insufficient power and this should be increased, the nose raised slightly. Re-trim after each correction.

(e) Small height corrections may be made with the elevators.

Lateral Level, Direction and Balance

a) Keep the wings level to prevent the aeroplane from turning off heading.

b) With the wings level prevent the aircraft from yawing by correct use of rudder.

c) Should the aeroplane swing off heading, move the stick in the direction necessary to bring it back into line. This movement should be co-ordinated with a little rudder in the same direction to maintain balanced flight.

d) Avoid flying with crossed controls. For example left wing down and right rudder to maintain heading. Notice the decrease in speed when flying out of balance.

At Selected Airspeeds

a) From cruising speed open the throttle another few hundred RPM and notice that if the attitude is held constant the aircraft will climb.

b) Prevent the climb by forward pressure on the stick and re-trim. The airspeed will now be higher than cruising speed.

c) Now reduce power below cruising RPM. Notice that if the attitude is held constant the aircraft loses height. Prevent loss of height by backward pressure on the stick and re-trim. The aircraft will now fly at a lower speed than cruising.

d) Progressively decrease the power until the aeroplane just maintains height at a low airspeed (the speed will depend upon the aircraft type). Reduce the speed by moving the stick back. When the airspeed has settled the aeroplane will lose height slowly although the power has not been altered.

e) Progressively reduce the speed step by step and note that power must be increased to maintain height until full throttle is required at the lowest possible flying speed.

f) Now practise Straight and Level Flight at selected airspeeds.

6

Straight and Level Flight with Flap

a)   Imagine the weather has deteriorated and you require to fly at Low Safe Cruising Speed. Reduce speed to within the flap limiting arc.

b)   Lower part flap (according to type but usually 15–20 degrees), add power to maintain height and re-trim. Notice the lower nose attitude for the reduced speed, giving improved visibility ahead and the increase in rudder/elevator effectiveness due to slipstream effect.

Instrument Indications

When fitted the following instruments will give these indications during straight and level flight. At this stage of training they should be used to supplement outside visual references –

a)   *Airspeed Indicator (ASI).* Because time is required by the aircraft to change speed there is a slight delay before the instrument settles to a new airspeed. This lag is appreciable and can cause inexperienced pilots to 'hunt the airspeed'.

b)   *Altimeter.* Under certain conditions thermal currents may cause height to vary although the airspeed and RPM are correct and the pilot must compensate for these variations during prolonged straight and level flying. In the case of a sudden gain in height the nose should be lowered and height lost by increasing the speed at that power setting. Similarly a small loss in height can be regained by holding up the nose. In extreme cases power setting adjustments will also be needed.

c)   *Engine Speed Indicator* (sometimes referred to as the Tachometer). Notice that a change in airspeed will alter the RPM, although the throttle has not been moved. Like a car running downhill a gentle dive will decrease the load on the propeller and cause the RPM to increase. A climb will produce the reverse effect. For this reason always re-check the RPM when the airspeed has settled.

d)   *Turn and Slip Indicator.* This is two instruments in one, so arranged because of the interrelation between directional and lateral movements of the aircraft. Notice that, if a wing is deliberately lowered while keeping straight on rudder, the ball (slip and skid) will move towards the lower wing, indicating a slip in that direction. If the wings are held level and the rudder made to yaw the aircraft, the needle (turn) will show a turn in the appropriate direction while the ball will displace away from the turn, indicating a skid outwards. Some Turn and Slip indicators make use of two needles, the lower pointer indicating Rate of Turn while the upper needle shows Slip or Skid. In

6

practice the two-finger presentation is similar in use to the more modern needle and ball instrument. Yet another presentation provides turn information in the form of a small, banking aircraft. Such an instrument is known as a **Turn Co-ordinator.** No pitch indications are given on these instruments although at first glance they resemble an Artificial Horizon.

e)   Vertical Speed Indicator (VSI). The slightest vertical movement of the aircraft up or down is indicated and becomes apparent as the stick is moved back or forth. The VSI indicates in feet per minute rate of climb or descent.

f)   Direction Indicator (DI). This instrument must be synchronized with the compass before it can be used for navigational purposes. Turn to the left and right when the DI will instantly measure the angular change of heading.

g)   Artificial Horizon. Notice at low airspeeds the model plane is above the horizon bar whereas the wings of the model cover the horizon at cruising speed. A gentle dive places the model below the horizon. Bank the aeroplane slightly and, in addition to the attitude of the model in relation to the horizon bar, notice how the pointer indicates the angle of bank.

h)   The Magnetic Compass. See Exercise 9, page 80.

7 Climbing

*The aim of this exercise is to gain height at a constant rate while
maintaining both heading and airspeed, and to revert to level
flight when the desired altitude has been reached.*

Imagine a motor-car moving steadily along a level road. When
it comes to a hill more power will be required if it is to ascend.
Similarly the aeroplane requires more power while climbing.

In addition to height and airspeed it is now necessary to
introduce a further measurement – **Rate of Climb**. As the term
implies this refers to the rate at which the aeroplane gains
height and is expressed in feet per minute. The Vertical Speed
Indicator (VSI) referred to in the previous chapter is arranged
to read zero in level flight. The instrument will also register
Rate of Descent in feet per minute and the dial is marked in the
manner shown in Fig. 37.

It is sometimes desirable to attain a specific altitude as
quickly as possible and to produce the fastest rate of climb it is

7 Fig. 37. The vertical speed indicator showing a constant height.

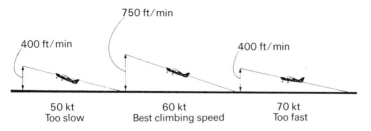

Fig. 38. The relationship between airspeed and rate-of-climb.

necessary for the aeroplane to perform under certain conditions.

As would be expected, maximum power authorized for the type of engine under climbing conditions will be required. This setting will be indicated in the Owners/Flight/Operating Manual for the particular aircraft and will be given in revolutions per minute (RPM). Often this information can be seen on a data plate in the cockpit of the aircraft.

In addition to the amount of power there is also an aerodynamic consideration. A climb attempted at too low an airspeed will produce a poor rate of climb and the engine may overheat because of insufficient cooling air. The rate of climb would also suffer at too high an airspeed. Somewhere between these two extremes lies the best climbing speed and by now it will be clear that it relates to a specific angle of attack which approximates to that giving the best lift/drag ratio (p. 8).

Unfortunately the speed demanded by the airframe for best L/D Ratio does not always coincide with that which is most suitable for the engine when running at high power and low airspeeds. It is therefore not unusual for the recommended best climbing speed to be slightly higher than the corresponding best lift/drag ratio speed.

Assuming the recommended best climbing speed to be 60 kt, the aeroplane would be able to *maintain* height at this airspeed using a small power setting. Under these flight conditions by opening the throttle there would be available to the pilot considerable extra power and it is this surplus horsepower **7** which is used to climb the aircraft. From this it follows that the greater the amount of surplus HP available from the engine the better will be the rate of climb.

A graph showing HP available/HP required is on page 226.

Flight Practice

COCKPIT CHECKS

a) Trim for straight and level flight.
b) Power set for cruising conditions.

OUTSIDE CHECKS

Look around and ascertain that no other aircraft are in the intended path of climb.

AIR EXERCISE

Entry and Maintaining Normal/Max Rate Climb

a) Check wings are level and open the throttle to recommended climbing RPM. Be prepared for the aircraft to swing due to slipstream effect and check the yaw with rudder.
b) Move the stick back and assume the climbing attitude using a point on the aircraft in relation to the horizon.
c) Hold this attitude until the airspeed settles, then if necessary move the stick slightly backwards or forwards until the best climbing speed is reached. Hold this attitude and re-trim so that there is no load on the stick.
d) Check engine RPM and adjust if necessary. Notice the instrument readings which should indicate a steady gain in height while the VSI will show the rate of climb. Notice the position of the artificial horizon.
e) Keep a good lookout. During a long climb turn gently from side to side in order to see over the nose of the aircraft.

Returning to Straight and Level Flight

a) At the required altitude move the stick forward and bring the aircraft into the level attitude.

7

b) As cruising speed is approached reduce the throttle setting to recommended RPM, checking any tendency for the aircraft to swing. Finally, when airspeed settles to that required, check engine RPM and adjust if necessary. Retrim for level flight.

Climbing with Flaps

a) Trim the aircraft at normal climbing speed and note the rate of climb on the VSI.
b) Lower optimum flap, hold the previous speed and re-trim. Note the reduced rate of climb.
c) Now reduce speed to that recommended for the climb with flap. There will be a slight improvement in the climb rate.
d) Raise the flaps and note the trim change.

En Route Climb

a) At maximum continuous climbing power trim the aircraft at the recommended speed for the en route climb.
b) Note the slight reduction in normal climb rate and the larger increase in forward speed.
c) For economy use the mixture control in accordance with the aircraft manual. This is the climb technique usually adopted during navigational flights.

Maximum Angle Climb

a) At maximum power select a higher than usual nose-up attitude and trim the aircraft at the recommended best climb gradient speed.
b) If recommended for the type, lower maximum lift flap.
c) Note the high nose attitude, low forward speed and rate of climb which will be slightly less than for a maximum rate climb. The aircraft is now climbing at an angle giving maximum obstacle clearance.
d) In a prolonged climb at low airspeed carefully watch the engine instruments for signs of overheating and either reduce power or increase the airspeed if this is evident.

7

8 Descending

The aim of this exercise is to lose height at a constant Rate of Descent while holding steady both heading and airspeed, and to resume level flight at the required altitude.

The descent is not only used to change from a higher to a lower altitude but it is the final manoeuvre immediately prior to landing. There are two methods of descending: (*a*) **Gliding** and (*b*) **Powered Descent.** Each method has its own particular advantages and applications.

In 'Straight and Level Flight' the function of the throttle control was explained. When this is closed completely the aeroplane is left without the thrust required to overcome drag and a force must be provided from another source in order to keep the aeroplane moving forward. The 'weight' component takes over this function and Fig. 39 shows how it is able to fill the gap left by thrust. Taking the extreme case, if the aeroplane were dived in a vertical position, 'weight' would be opposed and balanced by 'drag'. There would be little lift because of the small angle of attack during the manoeuvre, but the arrangement is unusual since under normal conditions thrust and not weight balances drag. In this position the aeroplane would lose height at its maximum rate of descent and very quickly exceed the maximum speed limit for the airframe **(Never Exceed Speed).**

Applying these principles to a more normal if less spectacular case, Fig. 40 shows the aeroplane in a 45° dive. It can be seen that weight is balancing both lift and drag. Although the rate of descent will be less than that experienced in a vertical dive, the aeroplane will still move forward under the influence of its own weight, or putting the situation into motoring terms, it will **8** 'coast downhill'.

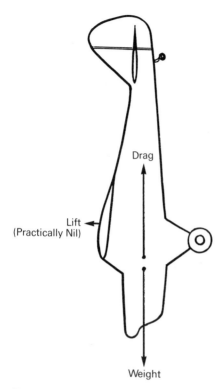

Fig. 39. Descending at maximum speed.
Weight is taking the place of thrust and, when the speed has settled, weight is balanced by drag.

The rate of descent would be high in a 45° dive but at a particular angle of attack the aeroplane will have the flattest glide path in relation to the ground. Such a condition will only occur when the weight is called upon to oppose the most amount of lift for the least amount of drag. In other words, the flattest glide will occur at the best lift/drag ratio angle of attack. This corresponds to a particular speed for the type of aircraft and any attempt to glide at a higher or lower airspeed will result in a steeper **Glide Path** (measured in relation to the ground). **8**

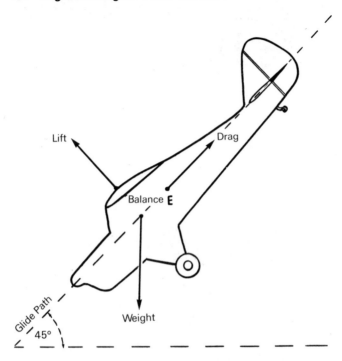

Fig. 40. In a steep glide.
Weight is balanced by lift and drag. As in Fig. 39, weight is the force pulling the aeroplane forward.

   If too high a gliding speed will steepen the glide path, for the foregoing reasons, an attempt to stretch the glide by holding up the nose will cause the aeroplane to sink because of the increased drag resulting from the higher angle of attack. This can be misleading to the pilot because although the aeroplane seems to be in the level attitude, the glide path is steep. Fig. 41 illustrates the effect of airspeed on the glide path.
   During a prolonged gliding descent the throttle should be half-opened every 500/1,000 feet to prevent the engine from cooling. With the throttle closed some engines are prone to carburettor icing under certain weather conditions and as a

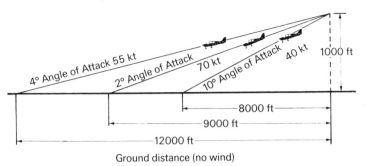

Fig. 41. The effect of airspeed on the angle of glide.
At 40 kt the aircraft sinks rapidly. At 70 kt height is lost in a gentle
dive. 55 kt is the best L/D speed for this particular aircraft.

safeguard against possible engine failure a **Carburettor Heat
Control** is fitted. When gliding this should be applied before
closing the throttle, thus checking its correct function (which
will be indicated by a small drop in RPM) and ensuring that the
mixture control has not been selected by mistake. Such action
would operate the idle cut-off and stop the engine.

There are times when it is necessary to control the rate of
descent within fine limits, e.g. instrument flying. The glide is
unsuitable under these conditions and the powered descent
must be used for the purpose. A speed below that related to
best lift/drag ratio is used so that with the engine throttled right
back there is a high rate of descent. Throttle is added in
sufficient amounts to give the desired rate of descent which will
be indicated on the VSI. This instrument was described in the
chapter on 'Climbing'. When the descent is too fast, more
power is added but if a faster descent is required power is
reduced. During these throttle adjustments the airspeed must
be kept constant on the elevators, i.e. rate of descent is controlled by the throttle and airspeed is controlled with the stick.

The Landing Approach

During the **Landing Approach** a flat glide path can be an
embarrassment for several reasons. Obstacle clearance is poor **8**

when crossing the airfield boundary prior to landing and in addition forward vision is bad because of the flat attitude of the aeroplane. A biplane suffers from high drag because of its 'unclean' design and this gives it quite a steep glide path so that restricted vision during the approach is usually because of struts, cowlings, etc., not approach attitude. The more stream-lined monoplane must have a means of increasing drag and **Flaps** are fitted to overcome the undesirable effects of too flat an approach.

Flaps are usually situated inboard of the ailerons and are of many designs some of which are shown in Fig. 42. The main

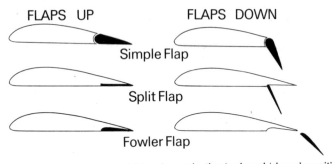

FLAPS UP   FLAPS DOWN

Simple Flap

Split Flap

Fowler Flap

Fig. 42. Three types of flap shown in the 'up' and 'down' positions.

function of the flap is (*a*) to increase the drag, thus giving a steeper approach without increasing the airspeed, and (*b*) to increase the lift at any particular speed. This also has the effect of lowering the stalling speed, an additional advantage during landing. In most cases the nose tends to drop when the flaps are lowered because the centre of pressure moves back as they are applied. There are a few aircraft which have a nose-up tendency but these are the exception rather than the rule.

The first 15°–25° of depression gives the largest lift increase and a modest increment in drag while further application increases the drag to a marked degree with little further improvement in lift. If it is necessary to raise the flaps while flying near the ground this should be done very gradually since some aircraft tend to sink as they are lifted.

Flaps are designed for use in the low speed range, consequently a limiting speed is recommended beyond which they should not be lowered, and once depressed the speed must not be allowed to exceed the limit. It is a common practice for the flap limiting speed to be shown as a white arc on the Airspeed Indicator.

Wind will influence both gliding and powered descent. Descending into wind the glide path will be steeper than that experienced in calm conditions while a downwind descent will flatten the glide path.

The Sideslip

With the introduction of flaps the sideslip is little used as a means of losing height more rapidly during the approach. Nevertheless not all aeroplanes have flaps and even when these are fitted the sideslip is a useful method of correction when landing or taking off out of wind.

There are occasions when an approach is too high and to pursue it would result in an overshoot. Without flaps to steepen the glide path other means must be found if this is to be avoided.

Surplus height could be lost in a dive but as a result the airspeed would be too high when the landing check was made. In other words the hold-off would be lengthy because excess speed will cause the aeroplane to 'float' for a considerable distance before touching down. In extreme cases the excess speed may cause the very overshoot which the pilot seeks to avoid. The effects of float following on a higher approach speed can be demonstrated convincingly and the higher speed is allowed to increase the longer will be the float.

In a sideslip height is lost without an increase in airspeed and herein lies its value. On page 35 under 'Further Effects of Ailerons' it was explained that the aeroplane will slip towards whichever wing is lowered and that a yaw towards the lower wing will follow. In a sideslip a wing is lowered and yaw is prevented with rudder applied in the *opposite* direction, e.g. **8** stick to the left, left wing down. Prevent left yaw by holding on right rudder or in other words, fly with 'crossed controls'. The aeroplane will now have a path of descent which is somewhere between the nose and the lowered wing and not straight ahead (Fig. 43).

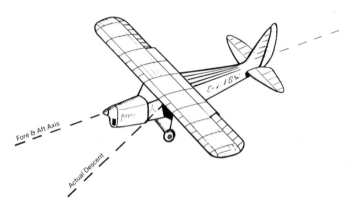

Fig. 43. The position of the aeroplane in a sideslip.
In this case the stick is held over to the left and yaw is prevented by applying right-rudder, resulting in the path of descent as indicated.

When in order to speed up the descent the angle of bank is increased so must opposite rudder be increased if the aeroplane is to keep straight. Maximum angle of bank will be reached when full rudder is applied to maintain direction and any attempt to increase the bank still further will cause a yaw.

It is convenient to practise sideslips at several thousand feet and to save time lost in regaining height after each descent some power can be left on to reduce the high rate of sink.

A velocity additional to the forward speed occurs during a sideslip. This is illustrated in Fig. 44 where it can be seen that there is a 'sideways' speed towards the lower wing tip. The actual path of descent is shown as a solid line and it will be appreciated that, since it represents the resultant of two speeds (one forward and one sideways), it must therefore be faster than the gliding speed before the sideslip is commenced. For

8

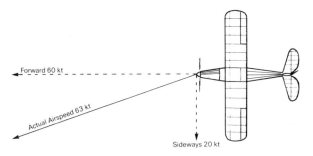

Fig. 44. The airspeed tends to increase during a sideslip because of the additional sideways velocity.

this reason the airspeed tends to increase during a sideslip and the nose must be held up slightly if the airspeed is to remain constant.

The sideways speed is greater than many experienced pilots realize and it is interesting to line up with a runway at say 500 ft and slip off the excess height. The distance travelled to one side of the runway during the brief descent is considerable. It is therefore impossible to effect a landing off a sideslip when the aeroplane is lined up with the landing direction, (*a*) because of the very considerable drift and (*b*) because at the end of the sideslip the aeroplane would more likely be over the edge of the airfield than on the landing area.

For a sideslip to be of value during a landing approach it is first necessary to line up the path of descent with the intended landing run by yawing the nose to one side. Because it is common practice to look along the left side during landing a sideslip to the left is preferable for the purpose of correcting too high an approach. Fig. 45 shows that a yaw to the right prior to depressing the left wing will make it possible for the machine to descend in a sideslip down to ground level without drift, when to effect a normal landing it is only necessary to turn the nose back into line with the landing direction while levelling the wings.

8

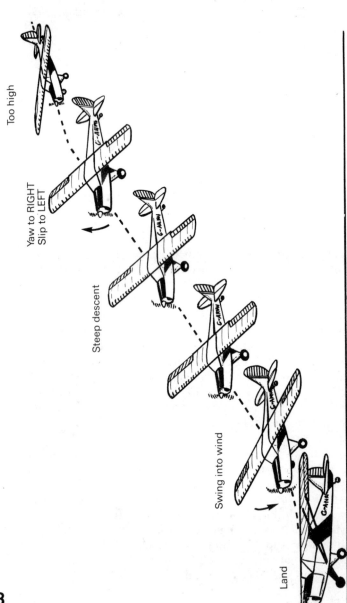

Too high

Yaw to RIGHT
Slip to LEFT

Steep descent

Swing into wind

Land

Fig. 45. The sequence of events when the approach is too high. The nose is held higher during the sideslip, thus maintaining the usual gliding speed.

8

Flight Practice

COCKPIT CHECKS

a) Trim for straight and level flight.
b) Engine set for cruising RPM.
c) Carburettor heat control as required.

OUTSIDE CHECKS

a) Altitude: sufficient to begin a descent.
b) Location: not over another aeroplane, in the circuit of an aerodrome, or within controlled airspace.
c) Position: check in relation to a known landmark.

AIR EXERCISE

Gliding: Flaps Up

a) Check below the aircraft. Apply carburettor heat. From cruising power close the throttle fully, at the same time keeping straight. Using the elevators, prevent the nose from dropping below the horizon.
b) As the airspeed decreases to near best recommended gliding speed, allow the aeroplane to settle in the gliding attitude and re-trim. Note the attitude of the nose in relation to the horizon.
c) Make any airspeed adjustments which may be necessary by slight backward or forward movement of the stick and re-trim. The aeroplane is now descending in a straight line at a steady rate and airspeed. Note the instrument indications.
d) Maintain a good lookout and during prolonged glides open the throttle at 500/1,000 ft intervals (according to temperature) in order to warm the engine.

Resuming Straight and Level Flight

a) At the required altitude open the throttle to cruising power, keep straight and adopt the straight and level attitude in relation to the horizon. Set the elevator trim control in the approximate position. Return the carburettor heat to COLD.
b) Allow the airspeed to settle and check the RPM. Re-trim if necessary.

8

Gliding: Flaps Down

a) Check below the aircraft. Apply carburettor heat. Close the throttle from cruising power and keep straight as before. Maintain straight and level attitude by backward pressure on the stick and hold this position until the speed has reduced to below maximum for flap operation.

b) Lower flap to the required number of degrees and allow the aeroplane to take up the 'flaps down' gliding attitude which will be steeper than before.

c) Re-trim at the correct airspeed and the glide path is now steeper. The model 'plane on the artificial horizon will indicate the steeper attitude. Also the airspeed is lower than before although there is a steeper nose-down attitude. Forward visibility is now much improved.

Resuming Straight and Level Flight

a) At the required altitude open the throttle to cruising power while keeping straight and bring the aeroplane into the level attitude. Return the carburettor heat to COLD.

b) Before the aeroplane accelerates beyond flap limiting speed, raise the flaps gradually and re-trim. If preferred trimming may be carried out in stages as the flaps are raised. When the airspeed has settled to that required check RPM and if necessary re-trim.

Powered Descent

a) Check below the aircraft. From straight and level flight select a lower power setting, say, 1500 RPM.

b) Reduce the speed some 10 kt below best gliding speed. Re-trim when the airspeed has settled and note the attitude of the nose in relation to the horizon.

c) The rate of descent is less than before and the glide path flatter. Because of the slipstream both rudder and elevators are more effective than in the glide.

d) Control the rate of descent by increasing or decreasing the RPM while the airspeed is kept constant with the elevators.

e) Resume straight and level flight as before, not forgetting to check that it is clear ahead of the aircraft.

f) Now practise the powered descent, using various degrees of flap.

g) With full flap notice the steep descent path when throttle is reduced and that considerable power is needed to maintain height.

The Sideslip – Entry and Recovery

a) At several thousand feet (with a little power on to reduce the rate of descent during practice), move the stick to the left and apply sufficient right rudder to prevent a yaw.

b) Correct the tendency for the airspeed to increase by backward pressure on the stick. Notice the path of descent is between the nose and the lower wing.

c) Steepen the bank and increase the rudder to keep straight and the rate of descent will increase.

Bank still further until full opposite rudder is required to keep straight, when any further bank will cause a yaw. This is the maximum rate of sideslip.

d) To resume a straight descent, level the wings, centralize the rudder and move the stick gently forward to maintain the airspeed.

e) Now repeat the exercise to the right.

8

9 Turning

The aim of this exercise is to turn the aircraft at a constant rate and height, or while climbing and descending. The turn is used to alter heading with reference to a heading indicator (magnetic compass, direction indicator, etc.).

Medium Level Turns

Unless it is forced into a turn a moving body of any kind will proceed in a straight line. For example a stone tied to a piece of string and swung around will describe a circle only because the string (which is held at one end) is pulling it towards the centre. Should the string break the stone will immediately fly away in a straight line.

An aeroplane behaves in exactly the same way as a stone in resisting a circular path. If an attempt is made to hold the wings level while applying rudder, the aircraft will skid through the air like a car on ice. To avoid skidding it is necessary to provide a force towards the centre of the turn as did the string in the case of the experiment with the stone. This is accomplished by inclining the lift (which always acts at right angles to the wings top surface, page 17) towards the centre of the turn. To do this it is necessary to **Bank** the aircraft, preventing slip or skid by application of rudder, i.e. the turn will be balanced. In contrast to older designs most modern aircraft require little or, in some cases, no rudder.

Lift is now made to provide two forces, a vertical one performing the usual function of supporting the weight of the aeroplane, and the other in a horizontal plane which acts as the 'string' pulling the aircraft towards the centre of the turn. This latter force is called **Centripetal Force** and the tighter the radius of turn for a particular airspeed the more powerful must be this force.

Fig. 46 shows that at any particular airspeed to tighten the radius of a turn it is necessary to increase the angle of bank so making more of the lift available as a turning force, i.e. centripetal force. If height is to be maintained during the turn more lift will be required and this is obtained by backward

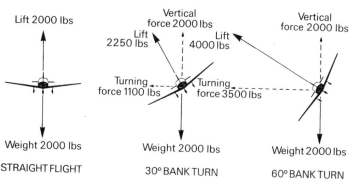

Fig. 46. The forces in a turn.
Lift must serve two functions: a turning force and a lifting force.

pressure on the control column, thereby increasing the angle of attack. This will, of course, result in a decreased airspeed and the steeper the bank (tighter the turn) the lower the airspeed. It will be seen from the diagram that in a 60° banked turn twice the normal amount of lift is required to maintain height. During medium turns, however, (25°–30° of bank) the decrease in airspeed only amounts to some 5 kt.

When the aircraft is turning the outer wing will move faster than the inner wing, causing unequal lift. Consequently in practice it will be found necessary to move the stick away from the direction of turn and back to the neutral position in order to prevent a steeper angle of bank developing than that desired.

The number of degrees an aircraft changes heading in a given time is known as the **Rate of Turn.** A change in heading of 3° per second (equivalent to a complete reversal of direction in one minute) is known as a Rate 1 Turn.

The rates explained in Fig. 47 are shown on the **Turn and Slip Indicator** in the aeroplane. The ball in this instrument denotes

9

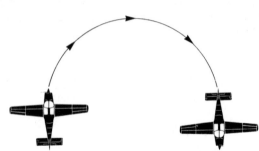

Hdg 360°   Hdg 180°

Rate 1 = 180° Turn in 1 min

Rate 2 = 180° Turn in ½ min

Rate 3 = 180° Turn in ¼ min

Rate 4 = 180° Turn in 7½ sec

Fig. 47. The 'rate of turn'.

whether the aeroplane is slipping or skidding and the needle indicates the rate of turn. In a perfect turn the ball should be in the central position and under these circumstances a full glass of water would not spill even in a steeply banked turn. This instrument is illustrated in Fig. 48.

Rate of turn is dependent upon the airspeed and the angle of bank. The higher the airspeed the greater the angle of bank required for any given rate of turn. An aircraft flying at low speed requires a small angle of bank for a desired rate of turn. The correct angle of bank for a Rate 1 turn may easily be calculated – 10% of the Indicated Airspeed in knots + 7 or 10% of the Indicated Airspeed in MPH + 5, e.g. Rate 1 turn at an IAS of 90 kt = 9 + 7 = 16° Angle of Bank. Rate 1 turn at an IAS of 500 MPH = 50 + 5 = 55° Angle of Bank.

Climbing and Descending Turns

At this stage of flying training, the student pilot will have practised climbing, descending and turning. It is often necessary to climb over a specified area in a series of turns or perhaps

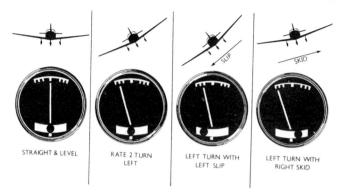

STRAIGHT & LEVEL   RATE 2 TURN LEFT   LEFT TURN WITH LEFT SLIP   LEFT TURN WITH RIGHT SKID

Fig. 48. The turn and slip indicator.
Dial indications are shown for four different manoeuvres, the right hand two being faulty turns.

descend towards an airfield which is to one side of the aeroplane. In either case a combination of the three exercises mentioned will be required. During a turn the stalling speed is higher than normal (Fig. 77, page 147). Should a stall occur during a turn it is almost inevitable that an incipient spin will follow. To guard against this possibility it is usual practice to depress the nose and increase the airspeed by 5 kt before commencing a gliding turn. Although modern aircraft are not prone to spinning without warning it is nevertheless prudent to carry out this procedure which stems from the days when aircraft needed little encouragement to spin.

These remarks apply to medium rates of turn but when a steeper bank is required it is important to increase speed by 10 kt or more to compensate for the increase in stalling speed as the bank is increased. During powered descents the speed may remain constant during a turn provided power is increased slightly, stalling speed being lower with power on than in a glide.

In a medium level turn it is necessary to move the stick away from the direction of the turn in order to prevent the angle of bank becoming too steep (page 75). During a descending turn there is no such tendency and bank must be held on throughout. The reason for this behaviour will be understood if a spiral

9

staircase is imagined. A little thought will reveal that both the inner and outer spirals of such a staircase will descend through the same distance from one level to the next. Whereas the inner spiral turns on a small, corkscrew-like path, the outer helix describes a path similar to that of a large coil spring. Relate this line of thought to a descending aircraft which is turning. The inner wing flying down the steeper path of the inner spiral will have a larger angle of attack than the outer wing which is moving on a spiral path of more gradual descent. The greater angle of attack on the inner wing is sufficient to override the higher speed of the outer wing thus making it necessary to hold on aileron during a descending turn.

During a climbing turn the aeroplane is, in effect, moving up the spiral staircase and the steeper inner path decreases the angle of attack below that of the outer wing. This may be experienced in flight, the aeroplane having a marked tendency to overbank when it is necessary to apply a little opposite aileron in the climbing turn, perhaps rather more than in a medium level turn. Spiral effect is illustrated in Fig. 49.

It will be remembered that in a medium level turn loss of height is prevented by a small increase in angle of attack, this in turn causing a modest decrease in airspeed (page 75). Similarly during a climb the addition of a turn has the effect of reducing the rate of climb (the steeper the turn the greater the reduction). Since the best rate of climb is only attained at the correct climbing speed it follows that during a climbing turn any attempt to maintain the rate of climb by increasing the angle of attack will have the reverse effect. Therefore during a climbing turn rate of climb is maintained by slightly increasing the power above that required for a straight climb.

Because the engine is delivering climbing power during the manoeuvre, stalling speed will be lower than normal (page 94) and it is therefore not necessary to increase speed during climbing turns.

The angle of bank should be limited to that required for a rate $\frac{1}{2}$ to rate 1 turn. Steepening the bank increases the demand on the power available for climbing, with an attendant reduction in rate of climb.

9

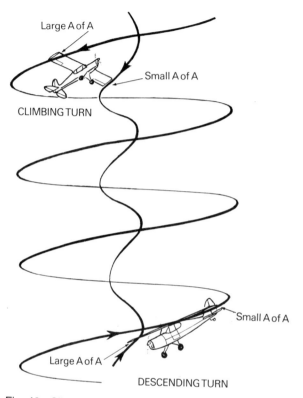

Fig. 49. Climbing and descending turns explained in terms of spirals.

Slipping Turns

Under certain conditions, e.g. forced landings, it is convenient to slip off height during a descending turn rather than a straight glide. Such a manoeuvre is called a **Slipping Turn** and, because the outer wing travels faster in any turn, a steeper angle of bank is possible than in a straight side-slip and height loss can be very considerable during the manoeuvre.

In principle the slipping turn is a gliding turn with too much bank for the rate. It is achieved by reducing the backward

9

pressure on the stick once the turn has commenced and applying a little top rudder but not to the extent that yaw in the direction of turn is prevented. From a position close to the downwind boundary of the field it is possible to lose height during a 180° slipping turn rolling out into wind and ready for a landing. Such a procedure is ideal when obstructions such as tall trees prevent a straight-in approach.

The Magnetic Compass

By now the student will have practised the various types of turn described in this chapter. It only remains to explain how a turn may establish the aircraft on a particular **Heading,** i.e. the angle of the fore and aft axis of the aircraft measured in relation to north. Heading is maintained on a gyroscopic instrument called a **Direction Indicator** and since it has no built-in means of seeking north it must first be synchronised with the **Magnetic Compass.** Before describing the magnetic compass it is necessary for the student to have a working knowledge of the properties of magnets.

Magnetism and the Compass Magnet System

Only certain metals are susceptible to magnetism and in general these are confined to the ferrous group, i.e. iron and steel. Not all steels can be magnetized and some stainless steels in particular are immune.

Briefly, metal is made up of a vast number of molecules. When the metal is not magnetized these are arranged in a haphazard manner. By one of several methods it is possible to rearrange these molecules in an orderly fashion all facing in one direction when the piece of metal will become a magnet. Magnetism may be of a permanent or temporary nature, depending upon the type of metal. Usually hard steel will hold its magnetism while the reverse is the case with soft iron.

A magnet can be in the familiar horseshoe shape or it may take any form such as a flat bar or rod. Whatever the shape, the two ends of the magnet possess different characteristics. Fig. 50

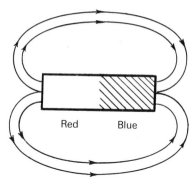

Fig. 50. The magnetic field around a simple permanent magnet.

shows that magnetic force creates a 'current' or field in a definite pattern around the magnet. The two ends are referred to as **Poles** and these in turn are labelled Red or Blue according to whether they are sending out (red) or receiving (blue) the magnetic current.

In so far as the magnetic compass is concerned the significance of this arrangement only becomes apparent when one studies the behaviour of two magnets together. Fig. 51 shows that when two magnets are placed in line with opposite poles facing, they are attracted and pull together, thus making a long magnet with the lines of force united into one continuous current.

Place the two magnets in the same position with like poles adjacent (e.g. red to red or blue to blue) and they will move apart. In other words, unlike poles attract and like poles repel and this is the fundamental principle behind the magnetic compass.

The largest magnet in the world is the earth itself and it is to the **Magnetic North Pole** that the compass needle is attracted. Unfortunately magnetic north does not coincide with true north as depicted on a map and the angular difference between the two is called **Variation.** Variation differs according to location and for reasons not fully understood it is changing slightly each year. Variation is shown on aviation maps and in the British Isles it is 7° W. in the London area and 9° W. of true north at **9**

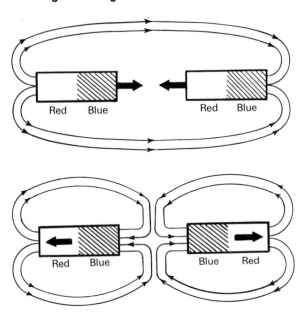

Fig. 51. The polarity of magnets.
Unlike poles attract – like poles repel.

Land's End. These figures refer to the year 1977 and they are decreasing at the rate of 9′ per annum. Not all variation is westerly and in the Pacific area, parts of the United States, Australia and Russia, magnetic north is east of true north.

The method of application when converting a true heading to a magnetic heading is easily remembered by the phrase 'East is least and West is best'. In other words deduct easterly variation from the true heading to arrive at magnetic heading and add westerly variation if this applies in the locality.

In a compass the needle is supported on a jewelled pivot; but here a complication arises: whereas the needle will balance in a level position in equatorial regions, the north-seeking end (red) will tend to pull down towards the magnetic north pole as it is reached while the blue end of the needle will tilt towards the magnetic south pole if this is approached. Fig. 52 shows that at

9

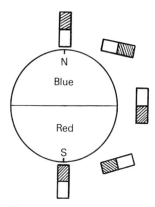

Fig. 52. The effects of 'dip'.

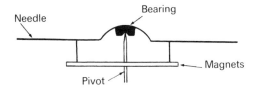

Fig. 53. A method of combating 'dip'.
The magnet is suspended below the point of the pivot.

the north and south magnetic poles the compass needle will attempt to stand on end. Clearly this tendency for the needle to dip is serious and unless compensated for in some way the compass would be rendered inoperative in regions north or south of the Equator. This fault is called **Dip** and it is largely corrected by suspending the magnet system below the pivot in the manner shown in Fig. 53 so that the magnets are able to act as a pendulum in opposition to dip, the system remaining practically level in all but extreme northerly or southerly latitudes when the use of the magnetic compass becomes impracticable.

Under certain flight conditions the magnet system becomes tilted. Then dip will pull the compass needle down towards the ground thus upsetting the compass reading until steady flight is

9

regained. For example, when the aircraft is on a northerly or southerly heading the magnet system will lie along the fore-and-aft axis of the aeroplane. Unless the wings are level dip will pull the north-seeking end of the compass needle towards the lower wing. Fig. 54 explains.

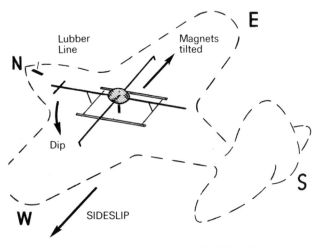

Fig. 54. False compass readings in N–S Headings.
A wing has dropped whilst flying on a northerly heading. A sideslip followed by a yaw occurs and this in turn causes the magnet system to tilt allowing 'Dip' to pull the compass needle away from magnetic north and towards the lower wing.

On easterly or westerly headings the magnet system will lie across the fuselage. Acceleration or deceleration will tilt the magnet system and dip will again pull the compass needle away from its true position. Fig. 55 shows that on east or west an acceleration will make the compass needle turn towards the nose of the aircraft indicating an apparent turn to north, the opposite occurring when the aircraft decelerates. When the speed is settled the needle will return to its true heading.

To overcome the errors which are caused by dip the following rules should be remembered when turning on to compass headings.

9

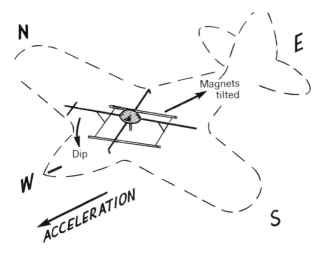

Fig. 55. False compass readings in E–W Headings.
On a westerly heading the aircraft accelerates and for a brief period the magnets are left behind, thus tilting the system. 'Dip' can now pull the needle away from magnetic north towards the nose of the aircraft indicating a turn towards the north.

Turning on to North from South, East or West

Roll out of the turn some 25°–30° before the compass reads north. Because the compass needle will have dipped towards the lower wing as the northerly heading is approached, the action of levelling the wings will swing the magnet system back through the last twenty-five or so degrees. It may be necessary to correct the heading with gentle turns.

Turning on to South from North, East or West

Roll out of the turn some 25°–30° after the compass reads south. Here again the action of levelling the wings will bring the needle up from the lower wing on to south.

When on north or south the wings must be level while checking the compass.

9

Turning on to East or West from North or South

As there is no lateral level error on east or west it is not necessary to overshoot or undershoot the turn by 25°–30° but allowance should be made for the time required to stop the turn. The roll-out should be commenced 5°–10° before east or west.

When checking the heading on east or west the airspeed must be steady otherwise acceleration or deceleration error will affect the reading in the manner already explained.

The errors described are at their maximum on N, S, E and W and they change progressively as the aircraft turns. For example, midway between north and east (NE) there will be some lateral level error and some acceleration and deceleration error.

The turning errors described refer to the northern hemisphere and the reverse effects occur south of the Equator.

All turns should be limited to a maximum of Rate 1 when using the compass. Turns of greater rate produce errors which render the compass inaccurate until the magnet system has been allowed to settle.

The Compass

The most common type of instrument installed in modern light aircraft incorporates a compass card which is attached to the magnet system so that the various headings appear to rotate behind a window past a mark known as the **Lubber Line** rather on the lines of a car compass only somewhat larger (Fig. 56).

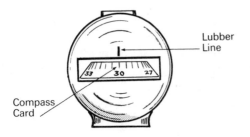

Fig. 56. Aircraft compass with rotating card.

9

Being a magnetic instrument of high sensitivity it will be appreciated that any ferrous metal in the aircraft will cause the compass needle to deviate from magnetic north. The deflection will vary as the aircraft turns around the compass and presents such parts as the engine or undercarriage at different angles to the magnet system. A **Compensating Box** is attached to the underside of the compass consisting of two sets of adjustable magnets, one correcting errors in the fore-and-aft direction and the other in the lateral sense.

The sequence of events necessary to correct the instrument is called a **Compass Swing.** It is repeated at intervals since there is a tendency for the aircraft's magnetism to change over a period of months or after it has flown through or near thunderstorms. Not all of the errors can be eliminated and a correction card will be found in the aircraft showing the error in various sectors around the compass. This error which is caused by the aircraft's magnetism is called **Deviation.**

It will be realized that because of variation and deviation there are three types of heading and these are listed below.

Name	*Abbreviation*	*Description*
True heading	Hdg (T)	The actual heading as it relates to true north on the map.
Magnetic heading	Hdg (M)	This is the true heading after the local variation has been applied.
Compass heading	Hdg (C)	This is the magnetic heading which, corrected for deviation, is set on the compass and flown by the pilot.

Flight Practice

COCKPIT CHECKS

a) Trim for straight and level flight.
b) Engine set at cruising RPM.

9

OUTSIDE CHECKS

a) Altitude: sufficient for the manoeuvre.
b) Location: not over towns or airfields, or in controlled airspace.
c) Position: check in relation to a known landmark.

AIR EXERCISE

Entry and Maintaining Medium Level Turns

a) LOOK OUT! Start on the opposite side to the turn, continue around the nose of the aircraft and end by looking behind in the intended direction of turn. Make sure no other aircraft are in the vicinity.

b) Bank by moving the ailerons in the direction of turn at the same time applying a little rudder in the same direction in order to maintain balance. Correct any tendency for the bank to steepen by moving the stick away from the direction of the low wing and maintain the nose of the aircraft on the horizon by slight backward pressure on the stick. The aircraft is now turning at an even rate without gaining or losing height.

c) Maintain lookout and check the instrument readings. The ball in the Turn and Slip Indicator should be in the centre. If it is not, a little rudder should be applied in the direction indicated by the ball in order to correct slip or skid. Height is adjusted with elevator.

d) To come out of the turn, look ahead, level the wings by applying aileron and rudder in the opposite direction to the turn. As the wings become level, maintain the nose in the correct position by returning the stick to its trimmed position.

LOOK AROUND FOR OTHER AIRCRAFT BEFORE COMMENCING THE TURN, DURING THE TURN AND PRIOR TO COMING OUT OF THE TURN. THE IMPORTANCE OF THIS CANNOT BE OVERSTRESSED.

Possible Faults and Action to be Taken

Nose high	Depress the nose to its correct position in relation to the horizon by slight forward pressure on the stick.
Nose low	Raise the nose by slight backward pressure on the stick.

9

Insufficient bank	Apply more bank and increase the rate of turn since it is too gentle.
Excessive bank	The turn is too steep and the bank should be reduced by moving the stick in the opposite direction to the turn.
Slipping in	This will be indicated by the ball in the Turn and Slip Indicator and a little rudder should be applied in the direction indicated which will always be in the direction of turn or 'bottom rudder'. During this correction the bank will tend to increase.
Skidding out	The ball in the Turn and Slip Indicator will move in the opposite direction to the turn and rudder should be applied in that direction or in other words 'top rudder'. During this correction the angle of bank must be held constant since it will tend to decrease as rudder is partially removed.

Climbing Turns

a) While climbing look around in the usual way before commencing the turn.

b) Open the throttle slightly and initiate a turn in the required direction but limit the angle of bank to that for a Rate $\frac{1}{2}$ to Rate 1 turn. Be prepared to 'hold off bank' rather more than for a level turn and maintain the correct climbing speed with the elevators.

c) Keep a constant lookout and note the instruments indicate a turn with an increase in height.

d) To return to the straight climb, look ahead and roll out of the turn in the usual manner while holding the climbing attitude.

e) Reduce power to climbing RPM and proceed with the climb at the correct speed.

Descending Turns: Gliding

a) From the straight glide look around and increase the airspeed some 5 kt by depressing the nose slightly.

b) Commence a turn in the required direction but be prepared to 'hold on bank'. Maintain the higher airspeed.

c) Notice the instruments indicate a turn together with a loss of height. Keep a good lookout while turning.

9

d)   To resume the straight glide, look ahead, roll out of the turn in the usual manner and slow down to the recommended gliding speed.
e)   Now repeat the exercise with the flaps down. The gliding speed is lower and to gain the extra 5 kt for the turn the attitude of the aeroplane is steeper.

Descending Turns: Engine Assisted

a)   From a powered descent open the throttle slightly and after the usual visual checks go into a turn without increasing airspeed.
b)   To tighten the turn open the throttle still further as the bank is increased.
c)   Resume straight descent by rolling out of the turn and reduce power to give the required rate of descent maintaining the airspeed steady throughout.
d)   Repeat the exercise using various flap settings.

The Slipping Turn

a)   Position the aeroplane in a glide on the base leg fairly close to the boundary of the airfield.
b)   Commence a gliding turn on to the approach in the usual way but steepen the angle of bank. Reduce the rate of turn by releasing some of the backward pressure on the stick and at the same time take off rudder but keep the aeroplane turning. Maintain usual speed for the gliding turn.
c)   Because of the high rate of descent allow plenty of height for the roll out from the turn.

Turns to Selected Headings, Including Compass Turns

a)   Fly west and find a reference point on the horizon on which to keep straight.
b)   Increase the airspeed with a sudden burst of power or by depressing the nose. Keep straight on the reference point and notice the compass card has turned towards the front of the aircraft during the acceleration indicating an apparent turn towards north.
c)   Now reduce speed by closing the throttle sharply or raising the nose. Keep straight on the reference point and notice the compass card has turned towards the rear of the aircraft during the deceleration

indicating an apparent turn to south.

d) Now turn on to east and notice the effects of acceleration and deceleration are the same as on west. In either case when the airspeed has settled the compass will return to its true reading.

e) Commence a Rate 1 turn to the left on to north and some 25°–30° before the required heading, roll out of the turn. The compass will now be within a few degrees of north and small corrections should be made as required. The wings must be level to obtain a true reading.

f) Keeping the rudder in the straight-flight position, lower one wing and notice how the compass card turns towards it. Level the wings and the card will swing back again.

g) Turn on to south at Rate 1 in either direction. Notice that at first the compass will give no indication of turn since the action of banking pulls the card in the same direction as the turn – towards the lower wing. Carry on turning until the compass card appears some 25°–30° past south then roll out of the turn. The card will swing to within a few degrees of south and small corrections can be made as required. The wings must be level to obtain a true reading.

h) Lower one wing as before and notice the compass card will move towards it as on north. Level the wings and the card will swing back again.

i) Commence a Rate 1 turn on to east or west. Notice the card gives an immediate indication of turn since the action of banking pulls the card in the opposite direction to the turn – towards the lower wing. When within 5°–10° of east or west roll out of the turn. The compass will indicate within a few degrees of the desired heading. Small corrections can be made as required but the airspeed must be steady to obtain a true reading.

j) Now try turning on the compass at a high rate. The instrument is of little use and on occasions indicates a turn in the wrong direction.

Note. When flying a straight heading, the pilot must not watch the compass continually. The aircraft should be kept straight on a distant object, and its heading checked by frequent reference to the compass.

Use of the Direction Indicator

a) Decide on a new heading and after the usual lookout checks, start turning.

b) At intervals watch progress on the direction indicator, and some 5°–10° before the new heading, roll out of the turn.

9

10   Stalling

The object of practising stalling is to familiarize the student with the symptoms associated with the manoeuvre and thus enable him to take the appropriate corrective action with the minimum loss of height.

Stalling occurs when the angle of attack is increased until the air can no longer flow smoothly over the wings, but breaks down into eddies with consequent loss of lift. This point is known as the **Stalling Angle** and the situation together with the attendant large increase in drag is illustrated in Fig. 57.

At the stall the centre of pressure moves backwards (Fig. 58) thus upsetting the balance of the aircraft and causing the nose to

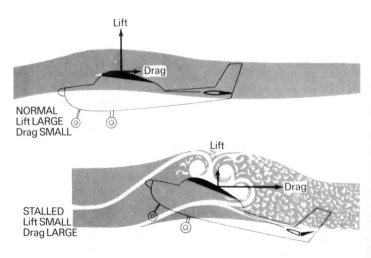

Lift

Drag

NORMAL
Lift LARGE
Drag SMALL

Lift

Drag

STALLED
Lift SMALL
Drag LARGE

Fig. 57. The airflow during normal flight, and at the stall.
In the second picture the nose is about to drop.

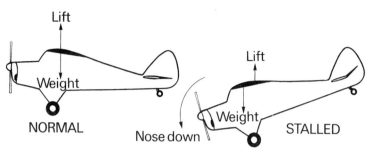

Fig. 58. Forces acting at the stall.
The backward movement of the centre of pressure upsets the balance
of the aeroplane and causes the nose to drop during a stall.

drop although the stick is held right back. Loss of elevator
effectiveness, resulting from low airspeed, is accentuated by the
turbulent airflow from the wings, which moves back to the tail
surfaces and over the elevators. Shortly before the stall many
aircraft give clear warning in the form of **Buffeting** (best
described as a shuddering of the aircraft). This will be felt
through the elevators via the control wheel or stick.

It is the practice on most modern light aircraft to fit a stall
warning device, usually in the form of a small sensor positioned
on the leading edge of the wing. At high angles of attack the
sensor (which consists of a small vane-operated electric contact)
switches on a stall warning light in the cockpit. Some instal-
lations include an audible warning, while another type in
common use takes the form of a simple whistle which becomes
vocal at high angles of attack. These devices are arranged to
give warning some 5–10 kt before the stall. More complex
aircraft have a **Stick Shaker** which behaves as the name implies.
Still larger modern aircraft incorporate a **Stick Pusher** which
automatically eases forward on the elevators when a stall is
approached.

Stalling can occur in any attitude since the angle of attack is
dependent upon the *relative* airflow. For example, if the aircraft
is flown too slowly with insufficient engine power it will
commence to sink, the relative airflow will approach from **10**

below the wings and the stalling angle will be reached as depicted in Fig. 59. Stalling will occur at any time when the wings are presented to the relative airflow at too great an angle.

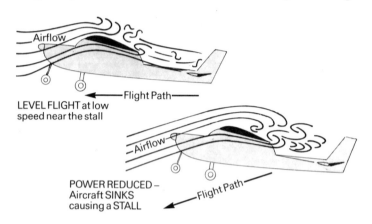

Fig. 59. Relationship of angle of attack and airflow.
Both A and B are in the same attitude of flight. While A is just below stalling angle, B is descending and the change in relative airflow causes a stall.

Factors Affecting the Stall

(*a*) Weight. This increases stalling speed. At any angle of attack a heavily loaded aeroplane must fly faster to maintain height than an empty one of the same type. This is because each square foot of the wing must support more weight and therefore requires a faster airflow in order to generate more lift. It follows that the stalling angle will occur at a higher speed in a heavily loaded aeroplane and other things being equal the higher the **Wing Loading** (weight supported in pounds per square foot of wing area) the higher the stalling speed.

(*b*) Power. This decreases stalling speed. The reason is two-fold. Firstly, with the engine running, the slipstream helps maintain a smooth airflow over at least that part of the wing which is within its influence. Secondly, it will be appreciated that, shortly before the stall, with power on the aeroplane will normally be flying in a steep, nose-up attitude. In effect the thrust from the airscrew will now be inclined upwards, contributing to the lift and relieving the wings of part of their load.

(*c*) Loading. This increases stalling speed. Not to be confused with the weight of an aeroplane which may be increased by the addition of passengers or freight, loading occurs during certain manoeuvres such as steep turns, loops and recovery from a dive. Under these conditions the effects of 'g' (which can be felt by the occupants of the aeroplane) temporarily increase the wing loading, and therefore the stalling speed is higher during these manoeuvres. Such a condition is called a **High-speed Stall.**

(*d*) Flaps. These are of many designs but broadly speaking first 15°–30° of lowering decreases the stalling speed. Further depression of the flaps will lower the stalling speed a little more but the main aerodynamic change will be an increase in drag.

The Fully Developed Stall

Due to manufacturing inaccuracies and particularly on aeroplanes with highly tapered wings it is usual for one wing to stall slightly before the other. The early stalling wing will drop first causing the relative airflow to approach from below, thus still further increasing its angle of attack and stalling that wing even more. Fig. 60 shows that concurrent with these developments the up-going wing partially unstalls because its relative airflow comes from above. If allowed to develop the nose will swing towards the lower wing because of increased drag on the fully stalled wing and weathercock action (described under 'Further Effects of Ailerons,' page 35). All the conditions for a **Spin** would then apply. An attempt to raise the wing with aileron would merely aggravate the situation since in the case illustrated the left aileron would be depressed. Such action would in effect still further increase the angle of attack. Likewise the up-going aileron on the raised wing would, in effect, reduce its angle of attack, aggravating the roll/yaw situation already mentioned. When a wing drops during a stall, yaw must be prevented by application of opposite rudder (in this case **Right**) **10**

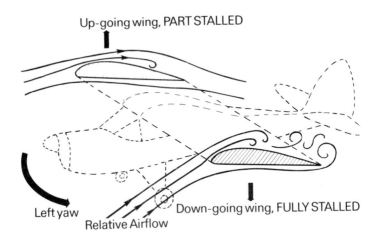

Up-going wing, PART STALLED

Left yaw

Down-going wing, FULLY STALLED

Relative Airflow

Fig. 60. When a wing goes down its angle of attack is increased
The reverse occurs on the up-going wing producing an unstable
condition since the up-going wing gains lift while the down-going side
is more fully stalled and less lift is produced

when the wings may be levelled after flying speed has been
regained. The full recovery procedure is outlined under Flight
Practice.

Preventing Wing Drop at the Stall

In order to prevent a wing from dropping during a stall, some
aircraft are fitted with **Slats.** These are small airfoil sections
which normally lie flush along the leading edge of the wing. As
the angle of attack increases the centre of pressure of the slat
moves forward, pulling it away from the main-plane. The
resulting gap between the slat and the mainplane (appropriately
called a **Slot**) allows high pressure air to flow from below the
wing and thus maintain a smooth airflow over the wing at high
angles. By fitting slats to the outer sections of the wing leading
edge (i.e. forward of the ailerons) the outer portions or wing
tips are made to stall later than those areas adjacent to the

fuselage, so maintaining lateral level during a stall. It is often possible to lock the slat in the closed position for such man- oeuvres as spinning and aerobatics and the behaviour of the device is illustrated in Fig. 61. Conversely it is sometimes the

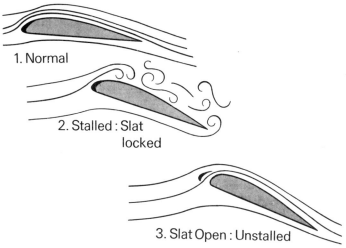

1. Normal

2. Stalled : Slat
   locked

3. Slat Open : Unstalled

Fig. 61. The automatic slat.
When unlocked it will open at a pre-set angle of attack under the influence of its own centre of pressure.

practice to attach small triangular section strips (commonly known as **Leading Edge Spoilers**) along 12″–18″ of the wing leading edge. Situated close to the fuselage these strips perform two functions when the wing approaches stalling angle –

(*a*) creation of turbulence and a breakdown of airflow over the centre portions of the wing thus allowing the un-stalled outer or tip sections to maintain lateral level.

(*b*) the turbulence generated at high angles of attack provides a pre-stall warning buffet.

An older and very effective method adopted by designers is to reduce the wing angle relative to the fuselage (**Angle of Incidence**) from root to tip, so that the inner portions stall before the tips. Such an arrangement is known as **Washout.** **10**

Flight Practice

Vital Actions 'HASEL'

Height – sufficient for the exercise.

Airframe – brakes off, flaps/slats as required, gyros 'caged'.

Security – harness and hatches secure. No loose articles in the cockpit.

Engine – fuel booster pump 'on', temperatures and pressures normal.

Location – out of controlled airspace, not above towns, airfields or other aircraft.

LOOK OUT – carry out an inspection turn.

AIR EXERCISE

Introduction

To induce confidence in his pupil the instructor will stall and recover thus demonstrating the gentle nature of the manoeuvre as it applies to light training aircraft.

Symptoms of the Stall

a) Apply carburettor heat then throttle back, keep straight and raise the nose just above the horizon.

b) As the airspeed decreases note the progressive ineffectiveness of the controls.

c) Continue the backward pressure on the stick until the pre-stall buffet is felt and the stall warning device operates. The aircraft is now close to the stall (Recover).

Stall and Recovery Without Power

a) Apply carburettor heat, throttle back, keep straight, and raise the nose just above the horizon.

b) Notice height and airspeed and continue backward pressure on the stick until the aircraft stalls. (Some types buffet shortly before the stall giving a clear warning.)

c) Recovery is effected by easing the stick forward thus gaining flying speed, when the nose should be brought up to the horizon and power applied. Notice loss of height which may be considerable. Near the ground this could be dangerous.

10

The Standard Recovery
(Stall and Recovery with Power)

a)   Proceed into the stall as before, noting height shortly before the stall.

b)   As soon as the nose commences to drop, open the throttle fully and gently ease the stick forward. It should not be necessary for the nose to go far below the horizon. Note that very little height is lost.

Recovery when a Wing Drops

If a wing should drop, opposite rudder must be used to prevent a yaw developing. Level the wings after flying speed has been regained.

The Stall with Power On

Practise stalling with a little engine power and progressively increase this. The more power used the steeper the attitude of the aircraft and the lower the speed before the stall. Recover as already explained adding extra power where possible.

The Stall with Flaps Down

With the flaps lowered and the engine throttled back carry out a stall and notice how rapidly the speed decreases as the stick is brought back. The stall will occur at a lower airspeed than from a glide without flap and the nose is likely to drop more severely. Recover as explained above.

The Stall with Flaps Down and Engine On

This exercise simulates the possibility of a stall during an engine assisted landing approach. As the stick is brought back the airspeed will not decrease as rapidly as in the previous exercise and stalling speed will be lower because of the engine power. Recover as explained above.

Recovery at the Incipient Stage

a)   Enter the stall in the usual manner.

b)   Check: yaw, airspeed and height.

10

c)   When the stall warner sounds or (if applicable) buffet is felt, apply full power, lower the nose to the horizon and prevent yaw with rudder. Note the height loss which should be minimal.

d)   Now practise this exercise from the turn, power on and power off, also with and without flap.

The High-speed Stall

a)   Go into a steep turn without increasing the power.

b)   Tighten the radius of turn by backward movement of the stick.

c)   Shortly before the stall buffeting may be felt. Notice the stall is at a higher speed than usual when power is on.

d)   To recover, ease the stick forward and increase the power. The ailerons will again become effective and capable of correcting any alteration in angle of bank caused by one wing stalling before the other.

11 Spinning

Spinning practice enables the student to recognize the manoeuvre, to take immediate action to prevent its development and to recover from this flight condition with a minimum loss of height.

It should be emphasized that, provided the recovery procedure is clearly understood, there is no need for apprehension when approaching this exercise.

The spin is a condition of stalled flight which usually occurs as a result of inexperienced handling of the controls. During a spin the aircraft is simultaneously pitching up, yawing and rolling.

The spin may develop from a number of flight conditions such as gliding turns at too low an airspeed, stalling or aerobatic manoeuvres, and can entail considerable loss of height. Some modern aircraft display a reluctance to spin even when deliberate attempts are made to induce the manoeuvre.

The sequence of events is as follows: shortly before the stall if rudder is introduced the resultant yaw will cause one wing to drop (Further Effects of Rudder, page 37). There will now be an upward airflow relative to the down-going wing. Consequently its angle of attack will increase and the wing will be fully stalled. The reverse conditions will exist on the 'up-going' wing. Because it is rising the relative airflow will come from above thus reducing its angle of attack and in the process the wing will partially or fully un-stall. The aircraft will slip towards the lower wing and weathercock action together with increased drag on the fully stalled down-going wing will maintain the yaw.

The aircraft will now continue to yaw, roll and pitch up (i.e. relative to the pilot, not the horizon). It is in a state of equilibrium known as **Auto-Rotation** and the complete sequence is illustrated in Fig. 62.

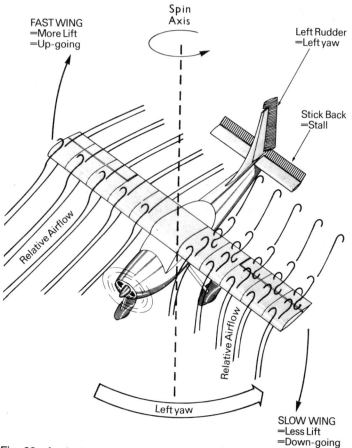

Fig. 62. Analysis of the spin.

The spin should not be confused with a spiral dive where the controls remain normal and the airspeed is high. During a spin the aircraft is at or near stalling speed and the ailerons and possibly the rudder are ineffective.

Spinning characteristics are dependent upon aircraft design and the distribution of weight around the spinning axis. The pitching fuselage and rolling wings each develop gyroscopic

11

properties. The student pilot need not fully understand these forces and it is sufficient to say that an aircraft with large heavy wings and a relatively small fuselage will spin at a fast rate and may be difficult to recover while a long heavy fuselage and small wings results in a slow spin rate and easy recovery. The loading of an aircraft (number of occupants, etc.) will affect its behaviour in a spin, tail heavy weight distribution having a tendency to flatten the spin and making recovery more difficult. Before practising this exercise it is therefore important to check that the aircraft is within its weight and balance limits for spinning. Some light aircraft are cleared for spinning in the **Utility Category** only. Usually this means when the rear seats are not occupied, thus ensuring that the aircraft's **Centre of Gravity** is forward. When the rear seats are carrying passengers, such aircraft are certified in the **Normal Category** when the resultant rearward shift of the C of G could very likely make spin recovery difficult, or even impossible. Furthermore, since the effect of an aft C of G is to assist the elevators in placing the aircraft in a high angle of attack, it follows that such aircraft are more likely to spin while flying in this condition than when they are, in fact, cleared for the manoeuvre.

Bearing in mind the effect of C of G position on the spin, it follows that other load in the aircraft, such as amount of fuel, will affect ease of entry and recovery, with some designs exhibiting a marked reluctance to enter the spin when the fuel tanks are full and the C of G is at, or near, its forward limit.

To recover, the original cause of the spin is removed by applying full rudder in the opposite direction to yaw as indicated by the turn needle. After a brief pause, which allows the rudder to start acting before its airflow is disturbed by the elevators, the stick is moved forward to unstall the wings.

Flight Practice

Vital Actions 'HASEL'

Height – sufficient for the exercise.
Airframe – brakes off, flaps/slats as required, gyros 'caged'.

11

Security – harness and hatches secure. No loose articles in the cockpit.

Engine – fuel booster pump 'on', temperatures and pressures normal.

Location – out of controlled airspace, not above towns, airfields or other aircraft.

LOOK OUT – carry out an inspection turn.

AIR EXERCISE

Introduction

Before an attempt is made to teach spinning the instructor will acclimatise the student by demonstrating a spin and recovery.

Entry and Recovery from Level Flight

a)   Apply carburettor heat, close the throttle and hold the nose just above the horizon. Approximately 5 kt above stalling speed, apply full rudder smoothly in the required direction of spin at the same time holding the stick right back. The aircraft is now spinning. (It is possible to count the number of turns by looking out at the horizon and watching for a known landmark each time it comes around.)

b)   To recover, apply full rudder in the opposite direction to the yaw. Pause, then ease the stick gently forward until spinning stops when the rudder control must be centralized immediately.

c)   Gently ease the aircraft out of the dive, level the wings with aileron and open the throttle as the nose comes up on the horizon.

The Spin from a Turn

a)   Apply carburettor heat, close the throttle and commence a gliding turn at a low airspeed by holding up the nose.

b)   Attempt to speed up the rate of turn by additional rudder and hold the nose up by further backward movement of the stick. Use aileron to 'hold off' the excessive bank caused by the additional rudder.

c)   The aircraft will begin to spin. Recovery in the usual manner.

d)   As flying speed is gained level the wings with ailerons. Ease the stick back and bring the nose into the straight and level position. Apply cruising power.

11

The Incipient Spin and Recovery (simulating a spin while turning on to the approach to land)

a)   Set the engine to approach power and hold the nose just above the horizon. Approximately 5 kt above stalling speed, apply excess rudder smoothly in the desired direction of turn, prevent the bank increasing with opposite aileron and hold back the stick until commencement of the spin.

b)   Recover: Stick forward. Power on. [The amount of power to be used in the recovery at the incipient stage will depend on the attitude of the aircraft. Provided that the nose has not descended far below the horizon, full power should be used as the stick/wheel is moved forward. When a steep, nose down attitude has been attained following spin entry, power should be added after the nose has started to rise. There is little point in using the engine to assist the dive.] Rudder away from down-going wing to check yaw.

c)   As the airspeed increases level the wings with aileron and return to straight and level flight.

Note. The Incipient Spin is a most important exercise and its practice will ensure that the pilot will be able to recognize the commencement of a spin and take corrective action before it has time to develop.

Important

1 **Power must not be used to assist full spin entry unless this instructional technique is permitted for the aircraft type (see the Owner's/Flight/Operator's Manual).**

2 **While aircraft differ in spin behaviour the degree of forward elevator movement needed to effect recovery will depend upon the state of the spin. A fully developed spin may require full down elevator while only part forward movement will usually be required after two turns of a spin or less.**

3 **Immediately prior to recovery the rate of spin may increase. This indicates that the correct recovery action has been taken.**

11

12   Take-off and Circuit to Downwind Position

The aim of the exercise is to fly the aircraft off the ground in a predetermined direction so that a climb can be commenced to the altitude necessary for the flight. The aim of the circuit is to position the aeroplane for a successful landing.

It is desirable to take off with a short ground run (*a*) to avoid unnecessary wear of the tyres and wheel-bearings and (*b*) in order to clear the far boundary of the airfield in safety.

Outside the perimeter of the airfield, buildings and trees must often be flown over immediately after take-off and in consequence a steep angle of climb in relation to the ground is a further requirement. It is with this consideration in mind that whenever possible the take-off is carried out into wind. One or more ground indications are provided at the aerodrome for the purpose of showing wind direction and these are listed on page 119.

How does taking off into wind make it possible to meet the foregoing requirements? It will be remembered that there is a minimum speed below which the aircraft will fail to generate sufficient lift for flight. On a light aeroplane the take-off usually occurs some 10 to 15 kt above this speed.

Assuming a take-off speed of 40 kt and remembering that it is airspeed (relative airflow) which generates lift, a 20 kt wind along the runway will provide half the required airspeed even when the aeroplane is stationary. In other words it will only be necessary to accelerate to 20 kt **Ground Speed** to attain the 40 kt airflow needed for safe take-off. The effect of a 20 kt headwind is shown in Fig. 63. If an attempt was made to take off downwind under the same airfield conditions the ground speed would reach 60 kt before the necessary 40 kt airspeed lifted the aircraft off the ground and Fig. 64 shows that the

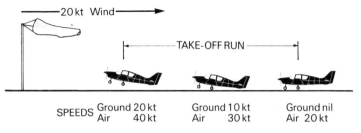

Fig. 63. The effect of a 20 kt headwind on the take-off run.

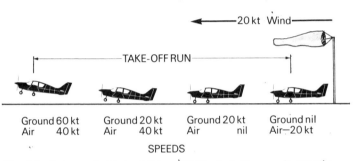

Fig. 64. A downwind take-off in a 20 kt wind. The run is greatly increased.

20 kt additional ground speed will require a longer run over the ground.

Once airborne the aircraft must not be forced into the climb immediately but the speed should be allowed to build up naturally to the recommended best climbing speed. From this point the climb away will commence.

Into wind or downwind the rate of climb remains substantially the same but the steepness of the flight path away from the ground will differ greatly. Assuming a rate of climb of 500 ft/min at a climbing speed of 60 kt and a take-off into a 20 kt wind, by the time the aircraft reaches 1,000 ft (two minutes' climb) it will be 8,107 ft away from the point of climb. This distance is in fact 2 min at a ground speed of 40 kt. A downwind take-off under these conditions would place the aeroplane 16,214 ft away from the point of climb when at a

12

thousand feet (2 min at a ground speed of 80 kt).

By drawing these two flight paths to scale and superimposing them on one another, Fig. 65 shows that in addition to a shorter take-off run, obstacle clearance is greater when taking off and climbing into the wind.

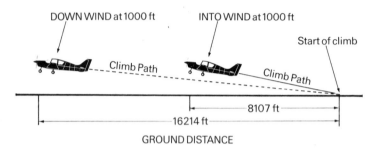

GROUND DISTANCE

Fig. 65. The 'climb away' to 1,000 ft drawn to scale.
Into wind the climb path is much steeper and obstacle clearance is good.

At low levels the wind is slowed by friction with the ground, becoming progressively stronger as height is gained. Since the 'into wind' condition entails climbing into an ever-strengthening headwind the angle of climb will increase for the first few thousand feet, whereas the reverse would be the case when climbing downwind. It should be understood that this effect is only noticeable under conditions of strong wind.

Taking off in a **Crosswind** presents different problems since there will be a tendency for the aeroplane to **Drift** sideways during the procedure. There are times when a partial crosswind cannot be avoided and steps must be taken to counteract the effects of drift in order to safeguard the undercarriage. Crosswind take-offs are a more advanced exercise which will be dealt with later.

Before any flight the engine run-up procedure outlined in Exercise 2 (page 28) must be carried out by the pilot. Usually this is conducted at the **Holding Point** (position near the beginning of the **Downwind end** of the runway) so that the engine can warm up during taxying.

Differences between Nosewheel and Tailwheel Aircraft

The nosewheel undercarriage has eliminated most of the take-off problems associated with tailwheel aircraft, partly as a result of the level ground attitude which allows the pilot an unobstructed view ahead as compared with the more restricted view along the nose experienced with many tailwheel designs, but also because of improved stability or resistance to **swing** during the pre-lift-off phase of the take-off. Tailwheel aircraft begin the take-off in the tail down/nose up attitude so that the propeller shaft is inclined upwards. A swing away from the down-going blade results from this geometry, followed by an additional swing in the same direction caused by gyroscopic forces from the propeller as the tail is raised to the level flight attitude. At this stage the student need not concern himself with the problem other than to realize that since it is in the level attitude throughout the early stages of take-off a nosewheel aircraft is not subjected to the two causes of swing peculiar to tailwheel aeroplanes.

The propeller causes two additional forces which during take-off create a swing in the same direction as those already explained. These are slipstream effect (page 52) and **Torque Effect,** i.e. the tendency for the aircraft to roll in the opposite direction to propeller rotation so that during take-off one wheel is pressed harder on the ground than the other thus adding to the swing through added rolling friction. Torque and slipstream effect are present in tailwheel and nosewheel aircraft alike but their influence on the take-off run is, in the latter case, negligible. The behaviour of the propeller during take-off is more fully explained on page 54 of Volume 2.

During take-off the differences between nosewheel and tailwheel aircraft may be summarized as follows –

1. Nosewheel aircraft are directionally more stable than tailwheel types.

2. Nosewheel aircraft being in the level attitude while on the ground allow the pilot an unobstructed view ahead.

3. Because of the level attitude it is not necessary to raise the **12**

tail during take-off with nosewheel designs.

4. Tailwheel aircraft are not prone to 'wheelbarrowing' (described on page 112).

5. Tailwheel undercarriages are generally lighter than comparable nosewheel designs.

6. Unless the undercarriage is retractable tailwheel designs create less drag than nosewheel types.

Because of the foregoing take-off procedure differs slightly as between tailwheel and nosewheel aircraft so that it is necessary to consider the two techniques separately. However before the take-off is attempted in any aircraft the pilot must –

(*a*) ensure that the aircraft is below its **Maximum Authorised Take-off Weight.** Obviously this will have been checked before starting the engine.

(*b*) ensure that the aircraft is within its **Centre of Gravity** limits (balance). In the case of most two and four-seat trainers it is almost impossible to load the cabin beyond its limits of balance, but this aspect becomes of importance in some six-seat touring designs and light twin-engined aircraft as well as large transport types. Like (*a*) this check will have been made before starting the engine.

(*c*) determine that the airfield length and conditions will permit the aircraft to take-off safely. A light aircraft operation from a licensed airfield will normally have ample room for the take-off. But when the strip or field is short and the ground is soft (or the grass is long) the Owner's/Flight/Operating Manual must be consulted to find the aircraft's **Field Performance** under those conditions.

Items (*b*) and (*c*) are more fully explained in Chapter 3, of *Flight Briefing for Pilots Vol. 4.*

(*d*) check that he is at the holding point for the correct runway.

(*e*) complete a pre-take-off check to ensure that the aircraft is in a state of readiness for flight. Known as **Vital Actions** these take the form of a printed check list when the aircraft type is complex. With elementary training aircraft it is more usual for the pilot to use the standard mnemonic shown at the beginning of 'Flight Practice' on page 120.

(*f*) obtain take-off clearance from the tower, usually over the radio but occasionally by visual signal.

Immediately clearance has been given taxi on to the runway without delay, since time wasted by indecision can inconvenience other aircraft waiting to use the runway. To ensure that a minor swing left or right of the take-off path does not involve leaving the runway the aircraft should be positioned on or near the centre line which is usually marked in a manner similar to a motor road.

The aircraft should be stopped briefly while the controls are given a final 'full and free movement' check (page 27, (*b*)). This is to ensure that the controls are free and (when fitted) the Auto-Pilot is disengaged. A reference point on which to keep straight should be found on the far boundary of the airfield. After a good look behind and ahead to ensure that all is clear the take-off may now begin.

Taking-off, Nosewheel Technique

The throttle is opened smoothly and fully while the aircraft is steered with the rudder pedals using the reference point on the far boundary. This point is of particular importance on grass airfields where the visual guidance afforded by the runway edges and centre line is absent. In aircraft where the nosewheel is of the castering type, i.e. not connected to the rudder pedals, inherent tricycle undercarriage stability aided by the aerodynamic effect of the rudder will be sufficient to maintain direction. When a swing seems likely to develop the throttle must be closed immediately and the take-off abandoned.

During the early stages of the take-off run the pilot should check the engine instruments to ensure that engine behaviour is normal and the expected RPM are being indicated, confirming availability of full power.

Immediately directional control is ensured a gentle backward pressure must be applied on the control column to remove weight from the nosewheel. This important technique is sometimes overlooked so that the nosewheel is subjected to considerable unnecessary stress during the take-off run. Furthermore **12** under certain conditions there may occur a development called **Wheelbarrowing.** In effect unless a backward pressure is applied during the acceleration prior to lift-off the weight of the aircraft is removed from the mainwheels or in extreme cases the mainwheels may leave the ground while the nosewheel remains in contact with the runway. Any crosswind existing at the time will cause the aircraft to weathercock or pivot around the nosewheel like an unstable wheelbarrow in a manner that can be both alarming and difficult to bring under control.

When lift-off speed has been achieved a further gentle backward pressure will **Rotate** the aircraft, i.e. raise the nose and increase the angle of attack to the point where lift is in excess of weight. The aircraft will then leave the ground. At this stage the airspeed should be allowed to build up naturally (i.e. without deliberately holding down the aircraft) when the climb can then be established. During this phase the pilot will most likely have flown over the original reference point so that a more distant object, possibly a suitable cloud, must be used for the purpose of maintaining direction.

Taking-off, Tailwheel Technique

In the early stages the student pilot almost invariably experiences great difficulty in keeping this type of aircraft straight during take-off. This is understandable since most aeroplanes with tailwheel undercarriages have a tendency to swing when the throttle is fully opened.

During the take-off a point on the far boundary of the field should be selected which can be seen along the left of the nose and the aeroplane should be aimed like a gun on that point. Provided the commencement of the take-off run is straight, little movement of the rudder should be necessary in order to maintain take-off direction. It is a common mistake to concentrate on opening the throttle a little at a time to the detriment of the rudder control and the throttle should be opened smoothly and fully in one movement.

As the speed increases the tail is raised so that the aeroplane is running along in the level attitude. This in effect places the machine in a more streamlined position, thus helping it to accelerate. At the same time the angle of attack is near to that required for take-off. Care should be taken to maintain direction while the tail is raised, since the fast rotating propeller takes on the characteristics of a gyroscope and in tilting forward its axis a force is created which tends to cause a swing. During the take-off run the controls will become more effective as speed increases and the tail would lift higher and higher with disastrous results to the propeller were the stick left in the original position used to level the aeroplane. Therefore, the level attitude must be maintained by progressive backward movement of the stick until a further gentle backward pressure will lift the aeroplane off the ground. During this procedure it is imperative that the aircraft is kept straight with the wings level.

Use of Flap during Take-off

On page 66 it was mentioned that the first 15°–25° of flap depression gave a considerable increase in lift and only a moderate rise in drag. Therefore it is common practice for the flap lever to be provided with a take-off position or **Maximum Lift** position. When the flap system is electric or hydraulic take-off setting will be marked on the flap position indicator.

Although the use of flap during take-off has little effect on most light aircraft, the technique is essential to heavier and faster designs providing these advantages over the flaps up take-off –

(*a*) The aircraft becomes airborne at a lower airspeed and therefore leaves the ground after a shorter run. This in turn means that particularly on a rough surface the undercarriage is subjected to less wear and tear.

(*b*) After becoming airborne climb path relative to the horizontal is steeper because although the rate of climb remains unchanged (or may even decrease slightly) forward speed is 5–10 kt lower. Fig. 66 compares the positions, one minute after lift-off, of two identical aircraft, one with flaps up and the other with flaps at the take-off setting. Using flap the steeper climb path increases obstacle clearance and is of particular value

12

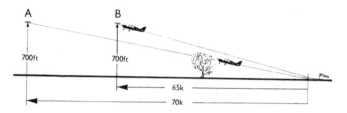

Fig. 66. Effect of flap on climb after take-off.
With take-off flap aircraft will reach position B after one minute. The lower aircraft, climbing flaps-up and due to reach position A after one minute is unable to clear the tree at the end of the runway.

when taking-off from a relatively small airfield surrounded by buildings and trees.

It should be realized that no benefit is derived from the climb out with flap unless the correct flaps down climbing speed is used, this usually being some 5–10 kt below the recommended best climbing speed in the flaps up configuration.

Not all aircraft derive improved take-off performance when using flap, and before using the technique pilots should consult the aircraft Owner's/Flight/Operating/Manual.

Crosswind Take-off

One of the disadvantages of runways is that landing and take-off direction is confined to them. Even a three-runway airfield can only provide six alternatives. On an airfield with a single runway it is possible to have a 90° crosswind. Naturally runways are sited with due regard to the prevailing wind directions in the locality but it is a common occurrence for the wind to be some degrees off the runway.

On some airfields a grass area is made available for light aircraft, these usually being more vulnerable to crosswind conditions than larger multi-engined types. Nevertheless, steps must be taken with all aircraft, big or small, to counteract the drift which must result from a crosswind.

Drift in itself is of no danger to an aeroplane when it is in the air and clear of obstructions. It is the transition from ground to air or air to ground which can be endangered by the presence of drift, subjecting the undercarriage and tyres to considerable side loads.

The aim is to carry out a normal take-off holding the wheels firmly on the ground, in the case of tailwheel aircraft by raising the tail higher than usual. In doing this care must be taken not to lift the tail too high, otherwise damage to the propeller could result from its striking the ground. During the early stages of the take-off run the control column should be moved towards the wind in order to prevent a wing lifting. When ample speed has been attained the aircraft is lifted cleanly off the ground in the certain knowledge that the extra speed will prevent it sinking and touching again with drift. As soon as drift occurs, the nose is turned towards the wind and a climb started with the flight path in line with the runway.

Throughout these explanations reference has been made to the runway. A crosswind may occur on a grass airfield which, for physical reasons, is confined to certain directions only and the same procedures are necessary and applicable.

Special Take-off Procedures

At a later stage in his training the student pilot will be introduced to the Short Field Take-off and the Soft Field Take-off.

Short Field Take-off

This method, as the term implies, is used when the aircraft must be operated out of a confined area. When the available take-off run is unknown the pilot will have to pace out the field, although care must be exercised since experience shows that with most people a pace is nearer two feet than three. Likewise the condition of the grass, or surface, and its gradient must be taken into consideration and the Owner's/Flight/Operating Manual for the aircraft consulted to determine that there is sufficient distance available for the prevailing conditions. The subject is described in Chapter 3, of Volume 4 in this series. As **12** already explained, whether or not flap should be used will also be found in the aircraft manual.

Soft Field Take-off

This technique is used when soft ground is likely to cause serious additional rolling drag. In extreme cases this could prevent the aircraft attaining flying speed. The aim is to start the take-off run with the control column almost fully back, thus removing much of the load from the nosewheel. When the elevators become sufficiently active to rotate the aircraft, the wings will be at or near flying speed. In some aircraft the back pressure on the elevators must be relaxed during rotation otherwise the tail may strike the ground.

After lift-off the speed should be allowed to build up before a climb is commenced.

Engine Failure after Take-off

With the general improvement in engine reliability a power failure at any phase of flight is very rare, the few instances occurring after take-off usually resulting from inadequate pre-flight inspection or incorrect cockpit procedure. Nevertheless modern pilot training includes various emergency drills so conceived as to enable the pilot to automatically carry out the correct procedure for safeguarding the aircraft and its occupants under all circumstances. Provided these procedures are fully understood and that temptations are resisted to act against the well-defined principles forming part of these procedures, in all but impossible situations it is feasible to land the aircraft with little or no damage and without injury to pilot or passengers.

Action to be taken will of course depend upon the circumstances at the time, e.g. height at moment of engine failure, obstacles ahead, landing surface available, weather, etc., but generally the following principles apply. Assuming the engine fails shortly after take-off –

(*a*) Immediately lower the nose to the gliding attitude.

(*b*) Make gentle turns avoiding obstacles and aim for the best open space within an arc of some 60° either side of flight path.

(*c*) Use flap as required or sideslip into the emergency area.

(*d*) When committed to the landing switch off the ignition, turn off the fuel and unlatch the doors.

On no account be tempted to turn back towards the airfield. Many pilots, some of them experienced, have yielded to this temptation often when there were available good open spaces ahead of the aircraft. A 180° gliding turn attempted at low height almost invariably results in an effort being made to hold up the nose and stretch the glide back to the airfield when a spin will develop from which it will not be possible to recover in the height available.

The Circuit to Downwind Position

The circuit embodies most of the exercises which have gone before this chapter. Particularly during training, the student will find that a good landing must be preceded by a good approach, and this in turn is dependent upon a good circuit.

Fig. 67 shows the complete circuit pattern which should be memorized. It is usual to fly around in an anti-clockwise direction, i.e. left hand, although, should there be an adjacent airfield or built-up area to avoid, a right-hand circuit may apply on occasions. The relevant signals for a right-hand circuit are shown in Appendix 2 on page 228.

The four sides of the circuit are known as **Legs.** After take-off the aeroplane is climbed to 500 ft when a climbing turn is executed through 90° on to the **Crosswind Leg.** When crosswind the climb is continued until local circuit height is reached. This is usually 800–1,000 feet above ground level. At this point the aeroplane is levelled and re-trimmed at a rather slower speed than normal cruising.

The pilot must now check that he is making good a path over the ground which is 90° to his take-off run, and if the wind is drifting the aeroplane towards the airfield he should turn away slightly. Continue the crosswind leg until at least a full width of **12**

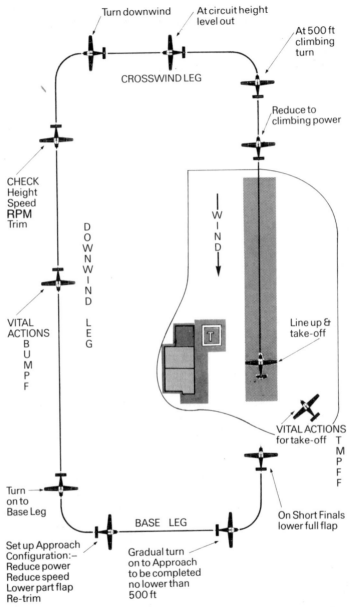

Fig. 67. The circuit should be clearly imprinted on the mind of the student pilot.

the airfield away from the take-off path, when a medium-level turn should be made through 90° placing the aeroplane on the **Downwind Leg**.

When downwind, check

(1) Height: 800 or 1,000 ft (according to local rules).
(2) Speed: Correct for circuit.
(3) RPM: Correct for circuit.
(4) Trim.

It is of prime importance that the downwind leg should be parallel to the intended landing path. Often the student pilot tends to converge on the field, thus placing the aircraft in a bad position for the next leg, and this common error should be corrected at all costs. When settled on the downwind leg go through the following vital actions –

B: Brakes off.
U: Undercarriage down and locked.
M: Mixture rich. Check for carburettor ice (i.e. with carburettor heat).
P: Pitch fine or in pre-landing position (pitch 'fixed' for most trainers).
F: Fuel sufficient for 'overshoot' on correct tank, electric pump 'on' and fuel pressure normal.

Like the pre-take-off vital actions this is a standard list suitable for more advanced aeroplanes and it should be recited in full even when all the items do not apply.

Airfield Signals Indicating Wind Direction

(*a*) The Wind Sock – a tubular fabric drogue which swings in the wind from the top of a pole. Its appearance gives an indication of wind strength as well as direction.

(*b*) The 'T' – a large sign painted white and displayed in the Signals Area. Sometimes arranged to swing with the wind but usually set in the correct direction by the control staff.

(*c*) Smoke. When the wind is too light to provide a wind sock indication, a smoke generator is sometimes used to give a **12** take-off or landing direction. This method can also be used to determine the position for aligning the 'T'.

(d) Runways. On airfields with runways there is often a grass area provided for light aircraft. In default of these arrangements a board is displayed near the signals area giving two numbers which refer to the runway in use. Should for example the figures 04 appear on the board the take-off must be made on the runway which has these numbers painted on its threshold. The two figures represent the magnetic compass heading of the runway to the nearest 10°. In this case 04 means a heading of 040°. The opposite direction would be 22.

Flight Practice

COCKPIT CHECKS

Vital Actions

T: Trim for take-off.
    Tighten throttle friction nut.
M: Mixture rich. Carb. heat 'cold' unless conditions are abnormal.
P: Pitch fine.
F: Fuel on and sufficient for flight. Electric pump 'on', fuel pressure normal.
F: Flaps up or take-off position.
Gauges and Gyros checked.
Harness and hatches secure.

(*Note:* Certain items such as 'pitch' and 'flaps' may not relate to some light aircraft. Nevertheless the pupil pilot should recite this list in full since it is a standard check suitable for more advanced aircraft which may be flown at a later date.)

OUTSIDE CHECKS

a) Position the aircraft so that aeroplanes taking off, flying around the circuit and landing can be seen.
b) Obtain clearance from the Tower and ensure no aircraft is on final approach before taxying on to the take-off area.

Into Wind Take-off (nosewheel aircraft)

a)   Line up on a distant point on which to keep straight. Check controls for full and free movement. Look behind and ahead. When clear to go, open the throttle sufficiently to move the aircraft at a brisk taxi pace.

b)   When sure the aircraft is running straight open the throttle smoothly and fully. Check the engine instruments.

b)   As the aircraft gathers speed ease back the stick to relieve the load on the nosewheel. Keep straight.

d)   Keep the aircraft running on its mainwheels. At the correct speed ease back the stick and lift the aircraft off the ground.

e)   Keep the wings level and allow the aeroplane to accelerate naturally to climbing speed then assume the climbing attitude. Find a new reference point possibly a cloud ahead.

f)   When clear of the field throttle back to climbing power (if applicable) and if necessary re-trim. Check pressures and temperatures.

Into Wind Take-off (tailwheel aircraft)

a)   With the aeroplane into wind, line up, using a point on the far boundary of the field visible along the left of the nose, check controls for full and free movement. Look behind and ahead.

b)   When clear to go, open the throttle a little while holding the stick slightly aft of neutral. When sure the aircraft is running straight, open the throttle smoothly and fully in one movement, keeping straight with rudder on the point left of the nose. Check the engine instruments.

c)   As the aircraft gathers speed, move the stick forward and raise the tail to the level flight attitude. Be prepared for a tendency to swing as the tail comes up.

d)   Maintain the level attitude by slight backward pressure on the stick until a further gentle backward movement will lift the aeroplane off the ground.

e)   Keep the wings level and allow the aeroplane to accelerate naturally to climbing speed, then assume the climbing attitude. Find a new reference point possibly a cloud ahead.

f)   When established in the climb, throttle back to climbing power and re-trim if necessary. Check pressures and temperatures.

12

Crosswind Take-off

a)   Line the aircraft along the required take-off run, select a point on which to keep straight and note from which side the wind is coming. Check controls for full and free movement. Look behind and ahead.

b)   Hold the stick towards the wind, open the throttle smoothly and fully and keep straight. Check engine instruments.

c)   Deliberately hold the aeroplane down and concentrate on keeping straight.

d)   When well above the usual take-off speed lift the aeroplane cleanly off the ground.

e)   Check the drift by turning the nose towards the wind.

f)   Establish the aircraft's track in relation to the take-off run and climb away as usual.

Short Field Take-off

a)   Having selected take-off flap during vital actions (or as recommended in the aircraft's Owner's/Flight/Operating Manual), line up the aircraft in the usual way. Check the controls for full and free movement. Look behind and ahead.

b)   With the brakes on, open up to full power, check the engine instruments, then release the brakes.

c)   Lift-off at the lowest safe speed (according to type).

d)   Keep the wings level and allow the aeroplane to accelerate to the flaps down climbing speed, then go into the climb. Find a new reference point.

e)   At 300 ft raise the flaps (if applicable) and increase the airspeed to the flaps-up climbing speed.

Abandoned Take-off

During take-off it is decided (due to part engine failure or lack of maximum power etc.) to abandon the take-off.

a)   Close the throttle.

b)   Apply brake keeping straight down the take-off path.

c)   If there is a danger of over-running the take-off area –
   Close the throttle
   Operate the idle cut-off
   Turn off fuel and ignition
   Turn off the master switch

12

d) Take firm avoiding action when there is a danger of striking an obstruction.

e) Advise ATC of abandonment at first opportunity.

Engine Failure After Take-off (Ex. 12E)

In the unlikely event of engine failure shortly after take-off –

a) Depress the nose to the gliding attitude immediately.

b) Close the throttle.

c) Look through an arc 60° left and right of centre and select the best landing area.

d) Put the aeroplane into the best open space available, using flap or a side slip to lose height if necessary. Switch off petrol and ignition when committed to the landing and unfasten the door latch.

NEVER ATTEMPT TO TURN BACK TO THE FIELD

12E

13 The Circuit, Approach and Landing

This exercise aims to develop the student's ability to maintain an accurate circuit pattern and to carry out a safe approach and landing.

The object of the approach is to position the aeroplane in line with the landing area so that a successful landing can be accomplished. The aim during landing is to place the aircraft gently on the ground within a pre-determined area and to complete the landing run in the correct direction.

Within the basic exercises required for a Private Pilot's Licence the take-off and landing usually present the student with most difficulty. In consequence during the flying course he will spend several hours 'on the circuit' practising these two exercises. The previous chapter explained the take-off and circuit as far as the downwind leg. When the downwind boundary of the airfield appears to lie at some 45° behind the pilot another turn is made through 90°, bringing the aeroplane on to the **Base Leg.** On the base leg, it is possible to assess the wind strength by the amount of drift away from the airfield and in some cases to correct this it will be necessary to turn slightly towards the field. At this stage the approach and landing will commence.

At a position which is dependent upon wind strength and the type of landing approach intended, power and speed is reduced and flap is lowered as required – here again according to circumstances. A further 90° turn is then made so that the aeroplane is in line with the landing run or, if there is one, the runway in use.

The aeroplane is now on the **Approach.** In effect this is a descent towards the airfield in the landing direction which will be indicated by one of the methods discussed on page 119. There are two alternative methods: (*a*) **Glide Approach** and (*b*)

13

the **Engine Assisted Approach.** A higher standard of judgment is called for in the glide approach and although the technique is now considered to be old fashioned, the pilot who practises the method at regular intervals has much to gain since it will develop his appreciation of distance, his ability to assess wind strength and its effect on the gliding angle. It also paves the way for a later exercise when landings must be made without the use of throttle, i.e. **Forced Landings without Power.**

The engine assisted approach is a powered descent and so any adjustments to the glide path can easily be made with the throttle. This method makes it possible to place the aeroplane on a particular area when landing and because of slipstream the rudder and elevators are more effective than during the glide approach. The powered approach is the method used by transport pilots since with larger aircraft it is important to touch down on the threshold of the landing area so that the full length of the airfield is available for deceleration and stopping.

A powered descent is slower than a glide and likewise the engine assisted approach is slower than a glide approach. The strength of the wind will affect the ground speed and this in turn will determine the length of ground run after landing so that whenever possible the landing is made into wind.

Mention has already been made of the effect of ground friction on the lower layers of air (page 108). While descending the wind becomes slower as the aircraft nears the ground, such a condition being referred to as a **Wind Gradient.** When approaching under these conditions the aeroplane will sink more rapidly during the last 50 ft or so from the ground. This will only occur when there is a fairly stiff breeze and the pilot is well advised to increase his approach speed slightly under these conditions and be ready with the throttle to increase power.

Whatever the method of approach, towards the final stages the pilot must be on the lookout for drift which can result from being slightly out of line with the wind, or to use the correct term **Crosswind.** A landing with drift will impose a severe strain on the undercarriage and there is a danger that the aeroplane will roll on to one wing tip on touch-down.

While an intentional **Crosswind Landing** is dealt with later, **13** small corrections are easy to effect by turning slightly away from the direction of drift, i.e. when drifting to the right turn slightly to the left and vice versa. A few degrees should be sufficient for the out-of-wind conditions likely to be met by the student pilot at this stage.

The Landing

At the end of the approach lies the problem and it is indeed a problem to most student pilots, yet without doubt one of the most satisfying experiences in flying is a really perfect landing.

Technique differs slightly as between nosewheel and tailwheel aircraft but common to both, the descent must first be checked by easing back the stick and bringing the aeroplane into the level attitude. The height at which **Round Out** is effected is the subject of much controversy amongst experienced pilots. Some talk in terms of beginning the check at the height of a double-decker bus whereas others refer to so many feet above the ground. The actual point is best demonstrated by the flying instructor. Executed properly the check places the aeroplane in the level attitude with its wheels a few feet above the ground. The next stage is dependent upon the type of landing. Naturally the aeroplane will lose speed as it glides parallel to the ground and if the angle of attack were held constant it would drop on to its wheels because of the decreased lift. As the aeroplane slows down and begins to sink again the stick is brought back sufficiently to reduce the rate of sink so that when contact with the ground is made the wheels touch gently.

The next stage will depend upon whether the aircraft has a nosewheel or tailwheel undercarriage. Assuming the landing is being made in a nosewheel type (Fig. 68) as soon as the mainwheels make contact with the ground, because they are behind the centre of gravity a pitch forward will occur, reducing the angle of attack and thus ensuring that the aircraft remains firmly on the ground. It is however important to maintain a little backward pressure on the control column so relieving the nosewheel of undue strain and avoiding the possibility of

13

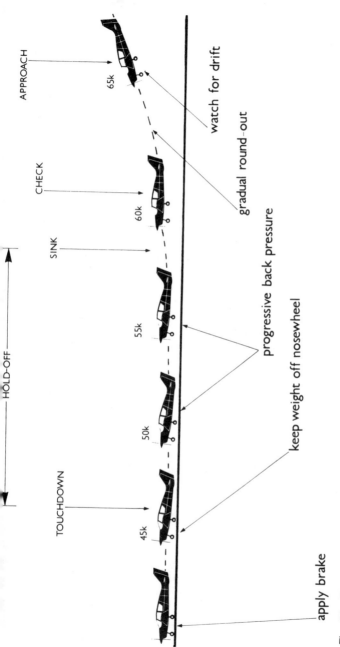

Fig. 68. Typical landing sequence for nosewheel aircraft.

13

wheelbarrowing (page 112). As soon as directional control is assured and provided the nosewheel is on the ground, brake may be applied to bring the aircraft to a halt. The aircraft is then taxied off the landing area, the flaps raised and (when applicable) the electric fuel pump is switched off.

Tailwheel Aircraft

With this type of undercarriage the mainwheels are before the centre of gravity so that on touch down there will be an immediate tendency for the angle of attack to increase thus lifting the aeroplane off the ground again in a nose-up attitude. It is therefore necessary to ease the stick almost imperceptibly forward as soon as contact with the ground is felt. The tail is held up in this position as the aeroplane decelerates, since to force the tail down would lift the aircraft off again. Such a landing is more common with large aircraft of old design and is called a **Wheel Landing** (Fig. 69). From its description it will be seen that the actual touch-down speed is relatively high since the aeroplane is virtually flown on to the ground at a moderate angle of attack.

The better method for light aircraft of the tailwheel type is the **Three Point Landing** – so called because in a perfect example the three wheels touch the ground simultaneously. The check is initiated as before but instead of allowing the main wheels to touch, the aeroplane is held off the ground as long as possible by progressively moving back the stick and increasing the angle of attack in step with the decreasing speed. When in the three-point attitude the machine will sink gently to the ground (Fig. 69). 'Gently' is the operative word and will only be the case if the wheels are near the ground during the final stages of the landing.

It is this last phase, the **Hold Off,** which demands a high degree of skill and, as is so often the case, practice is the only means of attaining it. The difficulties confronting the pupil are several. Surprisingly it is not easy to appreciate exactly where the ground is during the hold off and a simple but nevertheless valuable practice is to sit in the aeroplane while on the ground

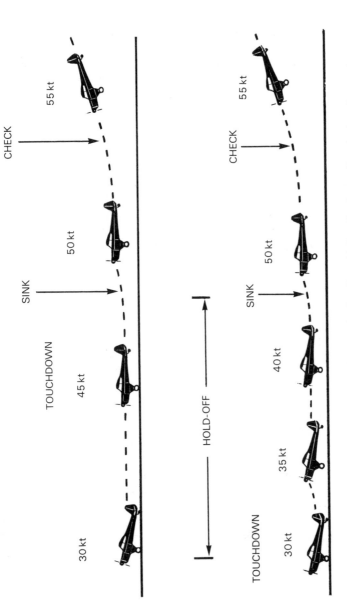

Fig. 69. (*Top*) A wheel landing. (*Lower*) A three-point landing. Notice the lower 'touch down' speed.

13

and really become accustomed to the appearance of the ground in the three-point attitude.

Throughout all landings the pilot must watch the ground along the left of the nose and the actual focal point is important. If the pilot were to look straight below he would probably fail to keep straight. The eyes should move back and forth during the hold-off period, ranging from a few yards ahead to the length of a cricket pitch or more away from the aircraft. In this way the pilot will be able to appreciate where the ground is in relation to the aeroplane and at the same time keep straight.

Touch-down speed is lower than that experienced in a wheel landing since the three-point attitude places the machine at a large angle of attack. On most aeroplanes this is just below stalling angle but with some of the older designs a stall is reached as the three-point attitude is realized. Whether the aeroplane is stalled or not largely depends on the length of the undercarriage legs.

The lower touch-down speed has the advantage of shortening the ground run. Care must be taken to keep straight while coming to a halt and it should be remembered that the landing is not completed until the aeroplane has stopped. Bearing in mind the low speed and lack of slipstream at this stage it will be realized that the rudder will be fairly ineffective and coarse use will be necessary as the aeroplane slows down.

Brakes should be used sparingly during the latter stages of the run. It is good practice to apply them intermittently so as to prevent overheating and possible 'fading' unless disc brakes are fitted, when the only danger from harsh application is the possibility of nosing over.

As a protection from flying stones, etc. the flaps must be raised before taxying away. This is particularly important with low-wing monoplanes where the flaps are near the ground.

Landing Difficulties

Experienced flying instructors have evolved a number of teaching methods aimed at assisting the pupil to overcome landing difficulties during training. Some of these are listed below.

13

During a Glide Approach

Watch the boundary of the airfield and if it appears to move down the windscreen during the approach the aeroplane is too high and may overshoot. More flap should be lowered. Conversely if the boundary moves up the windscreen the aeroplane is undershooting and the throttle should be opened and height maintained until the aeroplane is nearer the field, when the throttle should be closed again. The airspeed should not be allowed to decrease as the throttle is closed. Do not be tempted to reduce the flap setting during an undershoot since some aircraft sink when the flaps are raised.

During an Engine Assisted Approach

The same remarks apply but the adjustments will be made on the throttle while the airspeed is held constant. To make movement easier the throttle nut should be slackened a little.

The Round Out

It is better to start thinking about checking the descent at a reasonable height so that a gradual 'round out' can be executed rather than descend to within a few feet of the ground and then be faced with a sudden levelling out. Fig. 70 shows both methods and alternative 'A' is a much better proposition for the student pilot.

The actual height at which to initiate the check is difficult to define since a number of feet from the ground conveys little when viewed from the aeroplane. 'When the ground seems to expand around the aeroplane' is one description, while another which may help is 'when the ground rushes up to meet the aircraft so that something must be done to stop the descent'. Only practical experience can really convey the true picture.

Guard against bringing back the stick too quickly, otherwise the aeroplane will climb away from the ground, the angle of attack being too great for level flight at that speed. An aeroplane is said to **Balloon** when this occurs, the speed decreasing rapidly in extreme nose-up cases so that the hand must be kept on the throttle ready to put on power and gradually lower the aeroplane to the ground. On these **13**

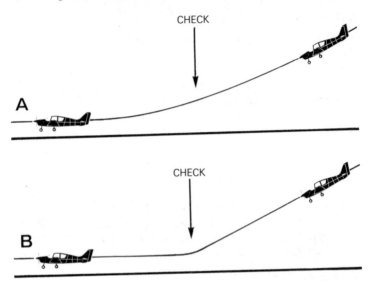

Fig. 70. Checking the descent prior to landing.
While method B is often used by experienced pilots, A is probably better and certainly preferable for the student pilot.

occasions power should be left on until the actual touch-down when the throttle must be closed immediately. On the other hand should there be insufficient landing area ahead, it may be necessary to fully open the throttle and 'go round again' for another attempt at the landing (described later in this chapter), and the flying instructor will advise his pupil according to the size of the airfield and whatever other factors may apply. The balloon and its correction is shown in Fig. 72, but during early training the pupil is encouraged to **Overshoot** and try another landing.

The Hold-off (Nosewheel Aircraft)

The relative ease with which a modern nosewheel undercarriage aircraft may be landed has, over a period of time, bred a generation of pilots who have lost the art of landing correctly. It

13

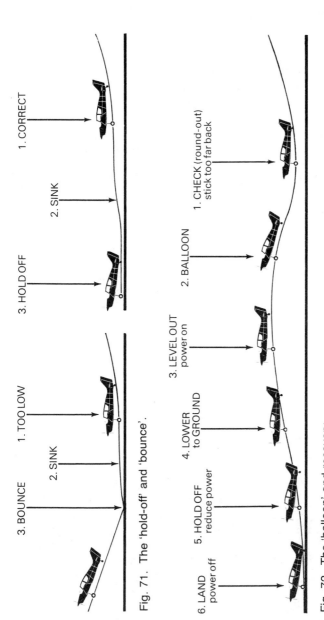

3. BOUNCE   **1. TOO LOW**

2. SINK

3. HOLD OFF   **2. SINK**   **1. CORRECT**

Fig. 71. The 'hold-off' and 'bounce'.

6. LAND power off

5. HOLD OFF reduce power

4. LOWER to GROUND

3. LEVEL OUT power on

2. BALLOON

1. CHECK (round-out) stick too far back

Fig. 72. The 'balloon' and recovery.

13

is, of course, possible to continue the approach to within a few feet of the ground, then bring back the control column, level the aircraft and wait for the wheels to make contact with the ground. Such an arrival (it cannot be called a landing in the true sense) must cause the aircraft to alight at a relatively high speed, hence the ever increasing number of broken nosewheel struts and the propeller/engine damage that follows.

The aim when landing a nosewheel undercarriage aircraft is to complete the round-out, reduce further sink to a minimum by gradually increasing the angle of attack as the speed decreases (i.e. by applying back pressure on the control column) when the main wheels should make gentle contact with the ground. Properly executed, the aircraft should be in a tail-down attitude with the nosewheel well clear of the ground.

After touch-down the back pressure should be maintained, thus allowing the high angle of attack to help slow the aircraft. Even when reducing speed causes loss of elevator power to the point when the nosewheel can no longer be held off the ground, back pressure should be maintained. Only in this way will unnecessary load and strain on the nosewheel assembly be avoided.

When the nosewheel is on the ground, and only then, the brakes may be applied progressively to help bring the aircraft to a halt.

The Hold-off (Tailwheel Aircraft)

If the point arrived at after the check is too near the ground there will be insufficient room to manoeuvre and as soon as the aeroplane commences to sink again the wheels will touch the ground prematurely. In a tailwheel aircraft this is bound to result in a bounce, a common error when learning, caused through aiming at perfection at too early a stage. Safety is the aim, perfection can come later. A few feet above the ground is ideal, there being sufficient room to allow the machine to sink again, thus providing a signal to begin the progressive backward pressure on the stick which gradually brings the aeroplane into the three-point attitude. Fig. 71 explains.

Recovering from a Bounce

The recovery from a bounce is a question of degree. A gentle one requires no action other than a second touch-down a few yards ahead. With tailwheel aircraft failure to be in the correct attitude before touch-down is more often the cause of bouncing than holding off too high. A heavy touch-down can, of course, produce a large bounce and here the same correction as that used for ballooning applies.

During the correction for both the bounce and the balloon, the aircraft *must* be kept straight and the wings *must* be level.

With a view to teaching the pupil the hold-off technique the instructor can (*a*) deliberately approach at a high speed so that the resultant lengthy float allows the pupil time to think, or (*b*) fly the length of the airfield at a low speed with a little power on. The pupils should hold the stick lightly while the instructor gently raises and lowers the aeroplane in relation to the ground. During this undulating passage across the field the pupil should watch the ground and say 'rising' or 'sinking' as the case may be. This method has produced excellent results with students experiencing difficulty in mastering the landing.

Crosswind Landing

To land with drift is to invite damage to the undercarriage. Furthermore, on aeroplanes with a narrow track a wing tip can touch the ground as the machine makes contact drifting side-ways.

There are two methods of counteracting drift –

1. The nose of the aeroplane can be turned in the opposite direction to the drift, so that its fore-and-aft axis is at an angle to the actual flight path.

2. A sideslip can be made in the opposite direction which will cancel or balance the drift.

Many pilots prefer the second method for light aircraft, although the first technique is normally adopted by transport pilots. It now remains to incorporate these drift corrections with **13** a landing remembering that there is a tendency to swing into wind which must be watched during the subsequent landing run.

The procedure commences on the approach and when drift becomes apparent the aeroplane is turned away from it. An engine-assisted approach is preferable but not essential. If necessary the angle of the nose in relation to the landing direction should be altered during the run in, so that the aeroplane makes good a track which will take it down the centre of the runway. Assuming a tendency to drift to the right, the nose would be held to the left in the manner shown in Fig. 73. The nose must be held in this position during the 'hold-off' period, otherwise drift would commence shortly before touch-down. If a landing were to be completed with the aircraft pointing in this direction it would run off the left-hand side of the runway. In practice the difficulty is easily resolved because shortly before touch-down the aeroplane is lined up with the

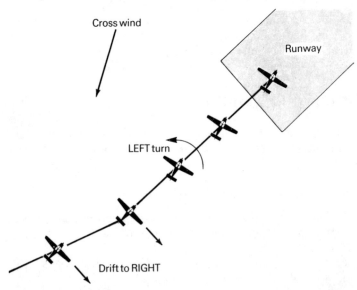

Fig. 73. Crosswind Landings.
Drift is counteracted by turning the nose of the aircraft towards the
13 wind.

runway using rudder alone; the skid which results from the flat turn is in the opposite direction to the drift and the two movements cancel one another (Fig. 74). Care must be taken not to line up with the runway prematurely otherwise drift will commence before touch-down, with the attendant risk of damage on landing.

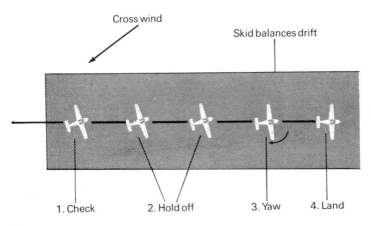

Fig. 74. The final stages of a crosswind landing (standard method). Lining up with the runway causes a skid which balances drift.

The alternative again begins on the approach, only in this method as soon as drift becomes apparent – say to the right – the left wing is depressed while keeping straight with opposite rudder. This will cause a sideslip but because of the crosswind the aeroplane will not drift in relation to the ground. There will be the usual increase in rate of descent during the manoeuvre and precautions must be taken to avoid an undershoot. The wing is held down during the 'hold-off' (in tailwheel aircraft a wheel landing is preferable to a three-point touch-down). The wings are levelled shortly before the landing but after contact the stick should be held into wind to prevent, in this case, the left wing from lifting. This is called the **Wing-down** method and the sequence of events is shown in Fig. 75.

In both methods because of the crosswind from the left there   **13** will be a tendency to swing in that direction due to weathercock action. Rudder and possibly brake will be required to hold the aeroplane to the required landing run.

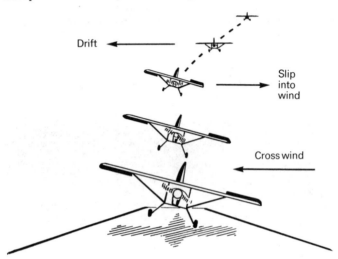

Fig. 75. Crosswind landing (alternative method).
A sideslip is used to counteract drift.

Use of Flap During the Approach and Landing

Some of the faster touring aircraft have cruising speeds that are too high for use around the circuit, consequently it is usual in these cases to apply part flap on the downwind leg. With most light single-engine designs, certainly those likely to be used for training, first application of flap is best delayed until the base leg. Amount of flap for first application will vary from type to type but a depression of 15–20 degrees would be typical.

On **Short Finals** when the landing is assured (i.e. it is unlikely that a **Missed Approach** or **Overshoot** will, for any reason entail 'going round again') full flap should be lowered. Many modern pilots seem reluctant to use full flap yet it is only in the final stages that a meaningful drag increase occurs and drag is of assistance at this phase of the landing providing better forward visibility, control, shorter hold-off and landing and a lower stalling speed. The only exception to this rule would be in conditions of moderate to strong crosswind when half flap will provide better handling.

The advantages of the powered approach are:

(*a*) better control as a result of slipstream effect over the rudder and elevators, and

(*b*) more precise control of the touchdown point since the rate of descent is adjustable through the throttle.

Considerations (*a*) and (*b*) require drag to be in excess of normal for the approach speed. This can only be attained in two ways –

1. by flying at a speed where the drag has increased due to a high angle of attack. This is known as **flying on the back of the drag curve** (see the HP Available/HP Required on page 226), and

2. by using the increased drag capabilities of the flaps.

For these two conditions to be met it follows that the approach speed should be lower than that used for best glide at best L/D angle of attack and that full flap must be selected.

Flight Practice

(The circuit is made up of exercises which have already been covered in previous chapters and only the approach and landing are detailed here.)

OUTSIDE CHECKS

a)   Altitude: 800 or 1,000 ft (according to airfield rules).

b)   Location: on correct circuit for runway in use.

c)   Position: on downwind leg with boundary of field just under the trailing edge of the wing.

13

COCKPIT CHECKS

Downwind Vital Actions

B: Brakes off.
U: Undercarriage down and locked.
M: Mixture rich. Carb. heat as required after checking for carb. ice.
P: Pitch fine, or in pre-landing position (pitch 'fixed' on most training aircraft).
F: Fuel sufficient for 'overshoot', electric pump 'on' and fuel pressure normal.

AIR EXERCISE

Powered Approach and Landing (Nosewheel Aircraft)

a)　Before turning on to the base leg continue flying downwind until the airfield boundary is well behind the trailing edge of the wing, say, forty-five degrees behind the pilot.

b)　On the base leg reduce power immediately and (i) reduce speed to that required for a powered descent, (ii) lower about half flap, (iii) open the throttle to control the rate of descent, and (iv) re-trim. Now slightly loosen the throttle nut.

c)　Look around and when clear to line up with the landing area open the throttle slightly and turn on to the approach. Alternatively if a little high depress the nose slightly and increase speed some 5 kt for the turn, reducing speed again when on the approach. Call 'finals' on the radio.

d)　The powered approach should be rather flatter than a glide approach. Control the rate of descent with the throttle and the airspeed with the elevators. If the runway begins to stand on end and the threshold moves down the windscreen, you are overshooting and must decrease the power. If undershooting, indicated by a flattening runway with the threshold moving down the windscreen, open the throttle slightly, maintaining the airspeed constant throughout. Look out for and correct drift by turning away from it.

e)　On short finals and when committed to the landing, lower full flap.

f)　Aim to cross the boundary and touch down on a predetermined spot. Check the airspeed.

g)　Watch the ground as it comes up along the left of the nose. Ease the stick back and check the descent.

13　*h*)　Keep straight and progressively close the throttle. Prevent the aeroplane from sinking rapidly by progressive back pressure on the stick until in a slightly tail down attitude the mainwheels make gentle contact with the ground.

i) Keep the weight off the nosewheel by maintaining backward pressure on the stick. Maintain direction on the rudder pedals then, as speed decreases and the nosewheel lowers to the ground, bring the aircraft to a halt with gentle application of brake.

j) Clear the runway and complete the after-landing checks – flaps up, fuel electric pump off (as applicable).

Powered Approach and Landing (Tailwheel Aircraft)

Sequence is similar to that adopted for nosewheel aircraft until (*g*) then –

h) Keep straight and progressively close the throttle. Prevent the aeroplane from sinking as power is reduced by continued backward pressure on the stick until in the three-point attitude, when it will sink to the ground on all three points.

i) Hold back the stick and keep straight by coarse use of rudder. Complete the landing run, then clear the runway and go through the after-landing checks.

Crosswind Landing

1. Standard Method

a) Turn the aeroplane on to the approach in the usual way. Keep a sharp lookout for aircraft on normal approach.

b) When drift appears, turn the nose in the opposite direction – into wind. Do not lower full flap.

c) Maintain the intended landing path by adjusting the position of the nose so that drift is counteracted right down to the hold-off.

d) Shortly before the aircraft touches down, yaw the aircraft into line with the landing path with rudder while keeping the wings level with aileron. Land in the normal way.

e) Bring the aeroplane to a halt, if necessary holding the stick hard over towards the wind to prevent the wing from rising. Correct any tendency to swing into wind using rudder and brake.

2. Wing Down Method

a) Turn the aeroplane on to the approach in the usual way. Keep a sharp lookout for aircraft on normal approach.

13

b) When drift appears lower a wing in the opposite direction – into wind – and keep the aeroplane heading in the landing direction with opposite rudder to bank. The aeroplane is now sideslipping into the wind and counteracting drift.

c) Maintain the intended landing path by adjusting the angle of bank as necessary while keeping straight with rudder.

d) Proceed down to the hold-off and level the wings just before touchdown. Concentrate upon keeping straight and during the landing run hold the stick over towards the wind. Be prepared to use brake to prevent a swing as the aircraft slows down.

e) Bring the aeroplane to a halt, still holding the stick hard over to prevent the wing rising and correct any tendency to swing into wind.

Glide Approach and Landing (Nosewheel Aircraft)

a) Immediately the runway threshold passes under the trailing edge of the wing, turn through 90° on to the base leg and, when sure the field can be reached close the throttle, reduce to gliding speed and re-trim.

b) Assess the wind strength by the amount of drift experienced and should this be great turn slightly towards the field.

c) Lower flap as required.

d) Make sure no other aeroplane is ahead or below and at about 500 ft execute a gliding turn on to the approach. Resume gliding speed and the aeroplane should have a straight-in approach from approximately 400 ft. Dependent on the wind strength lower the flaps still further. Call 'finals' on the radio.

e) Lookout for drift and correct by turning in the opposite direction to it.

f) With the hand on the throttle, watch the ground as it comes up along the left of the nose. At the correct height move the stick back and check the descent, thus making the aeroplane glide a few feet above the ground.

g) Keep straight and prevent a rapid sink with progressive backward pressure on the stick until in a slightly tail down attitude the main wheels make gentle contact with the ground.

h) Keep the weight off the nosewheel by maintaining backward pressure on the stick. Maintain direction on the rudder pedals then, as speed decreases and the nosewheel lowers to the ground, bring the aircraft to a halt with gentle application of brake.

13 *i*) Clear the runway and complete the after-landing checks.

Glide Approach and Landing (Tailwheel Aircraft)

Sequence is similar to nosewheel techniques until (*f*) then –

g)   Keep straight and as the aircraft begins to sink again ease back the stick progressively until in the three-point attitude, when it will sink gently to the ground on all three points.

h)   Hold the stick back and keep straight with coarse use of rudder. As the aircraft slows down apply the brakes gently and bring the aeroplane to a halt. Clear the runway and compete the after-landing checks.

Short Landing (*See* Ex. 17b, page 176

Flapless Landing

a)   Establish an approach at the correct flaps up speed.

b)   At the correct height check the descent in the usual way. Note the prolonged hold-off and the tendency to float.

c)   Be prepared for a longer than usual ground run.

Wheel Landing (Tailwheel Aircraft)

a)   Complete the approach in the usual way and carry out the check at the same height as in an engine assisted approach.

b)   Do not hold off but allow the aeroplane to sink slowly on to its main wheels in the level attitude. Immediately the wheels touch, slightly relax the backward pressure on the stick and hold aeroplane in the tail-up attitude as if in a take-off. This is a relaxation of pressure rather than a deliberate movement.

c)   Do not attempt to force the tail down but allow the aeroplane to decelerate, when it will sink of its own accord. The brakes must not be used until the tail is down.

Bad Visibility Circuit (*See* page 175)

Going Round Again

a)   Open the throttle smoothly and fully and prevent the nose from moving up sharply. Be prepared for a change of trim necessitating a heavy load on the stick on some aircraft. Keep straight.

b)   If the flaps are down, trim to correct climbing speed for this condition. Do not raise the flaps below 300 ft and then only in stages. Re-trim after each reduction in flap angle.

13

14 First Solo

The student pilot's first solo flight is certainly one of the most memorable and rewarding experiences in flying training. It is from this stage that the pupil takes his first steps as a pilot in his own right.

All the previous exercises have been leading to the point when the instructor climbs out of the aircraft and sends his pupil around the circuit on his own for the first time. Clearly before this step is taken the flying instructor will be satisfied that his pupil can not only take off, fly around the circuit and land, but also that he can deal with such eventualities as

1. Recovery from a misjudged landing.
2. Overshoot procedure.
3. Engine failure after take-off.

A number of successful landings is usually required by the instructor during the pre-solo check, and safety rather than perfection is expected of the pupil. An indifferent landing sensibly corrected is a sure indication that the pupil is fully aware of the events taking place throughout the manoeuvre.

Most pupils feel ready for solo before their instructors are prepared to send them and as their standard of flying improves the event is eagerly awaited by both parties. Pupils are often told to expect the aircraft to take off after a shorter run once the instructor is out of the cockpit, but in practice the difference is not easy for the pupil to appreciate and in any case it is so slight that it is of no consequence.

The take-off, circuit and landing should be flown as if the flying instructor were in his usual place and the pupil is usually so occupied with his own thoughts that he has little time to reflect on the vacant seat in the aircraft. For the first solo most instructors require the pupil to complete one circuit and landing only, but the pupil should not hesitate to 'go round again' if he is not happy with the landing or should he feel that an overshoot is likely.

It is particularly important that the pupil should maintain a good lookout since he is now on his own without an additional pair of eyes to warn him of the approach of another aircraft.

It is generally accepted that the pupil learns most about flying when he is on his own although it is equally true to say that long periods of solo without supervision are often the cause of bad habits being formed. For this reason after first solo the student's flying will be punctuated with dual checks when any handling faults will be brought to his attention and corrected.

When the time comes for the instructor to climb out of the aircraft he will stow his safety harness so that it cannot interfere with the controls. It is then for the pupil to enjoy this never-to-be-repeated occasion. For there can only be one first solo.

Consolidation Period

Following the first solo it is common practice to consolidate all that has been learned during the course. Early solo flights are punctuated with frequent checks by the flying instructor until the pupil is ready to leave the circuit on his own for the purpose of practising some of the upper air exercises. Before he is allowed to do this he will be taught –

1. The correct leaving and circuit joining procedures.
2. The locality of any restricted airspace within the training area.
3. Turns on to a particular heading and how to maintain that heading.
4. The ability to obtain a Magnetic Bearing (QDM) in the event of his requiring navigational assistance while returning to the airfield.

With this consolidation period should come improvements in skill and increased confidence when undertaking the remaining exercises required to complete the PPL course.

14

15 Advanced Turning

The aim of this exercise is to turn at a high angle of bank and obtain maximum turning performance. The manoeuvre also enables the pilot to see directly below the aircraft.

The steep turn is a development of the medium turn which was explained in Exercise 9. Exactly the same principles apply, but there are additional factors to be considered.

During any turn lift must be increased to provide a turning force in addition to its usual function – opposing weight. While the increase is small at gentle angles of bank, twice normal lift is required in order to maintain height during a turn with a 60° angle of bank. Beyond 60° the demand for more lift increases rapidly and at just over 84° ten times more than usual is needed to avoid loss of height. The aeroplane would then be turning at a very high rate (Fig. 76).

A force causes an equal and opposite reaction. For example, when a rifle is fired, there is a kick back in the opposite direction to the line of fire. During turns there is a reaction

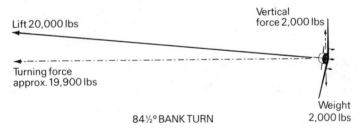

Lift 20,000 lbs

Vertical force 2,000 lbs

Turning force approx. 19,900 lbs

84½° BANK TURN

Weight 2,000 lbs

Fig. 76. Steep turns.
At this angle of bank, ten times normal lift is required, and this is usually beyond the capabilities of most light aircraft because of their limited engine power.

known as **Centrifugal Reaction,** often incorrectly referred to as 'Centrifugal Force'. Like the kick experienced when firing a rifle, it is the reaction to the force turning the aeroplane **(Centripetal Force)** and, when the aeroplane is permitted to fly on a straight path, centrifugal reaction disappears. Nevertheless this reaction is important to pilot and aeroplane since both body and machine are subjected to an increased loading. In a correctly executed turn at 84¼° angle of bank a 10-stone man would exert a force in his seat of 100 stones!

Putting this into other terms centrifugal reaction results from pilot and aeroplane resisting the turn while attempting to obey the law of nature which demands that an object must move on a straight path unless diverted by some exterior force. When, in this case a turning force is applied, there is an equal and opposite reaction and during turns such a reaction takes the form of loading.

On page 95 under Stalling it was mentioned that one of the factors affecting stalling speed is loading. Fig. 77 shows the increased loading at different angles of bank together with the attendant increase in stalling speed. A graph showing the increase in loading with bank is on page 224.

The wings will stall at the same angle of attack as in straight flight but, because of loading, the speed will be higher and a steep turn is an excellent means of demonstrating the high-speed

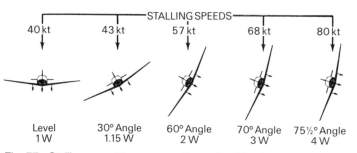

Fig. 77. Stalling speed increases with angle of bank.
The steeper the angle of bank, the greater the loading and consequently the higher the stalling speed. From 74½° angle of bank a further 10° will increase the loading from 4 to 10 times.

15

stall referred to on page 95. During any manoeuvre which increases loading, such as a steep turn, to produce the extra lift required speed will be higher than normal for any given angle of attack. Conversely, if speed is not increased, the angle of attack must be greater to produce the extra lift necessary under loading conditions. Since an increase in angle of attack means an increase in drag, more power will be required to overcome the drag in a steep turn, and in practice the steeper the angle of bank, the more power required. So far as light aeroplanes are concerned 65° bank is usually the maximum attainable without loss of height, this limit being dictated by the engine power available to overcome the high drag. In high-speed aircraft the limiting factor is usually the pilot who will 'black out' when the loading is beyond his physical capabilities.

The radius of turn is dependent upon the angle of bank and the airspeed. Assuming a constant angle of bank, the higher the speed the larger the radius. This is explained in Fig. 78.

Because of the momentum of the aeroplane it is possible to exceed the maximum angle of bank for level turns for brief periods. Such a manoeuvre is not a correct turn and cannot be sustained without loss of height.

Because of the number of variable factors involved the student is apt to become confused with the principles relating to

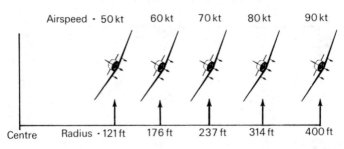

Fig. 78. Relationship of radius of turn to airspeed for a 61° angle of bank.
At a constant angle of bank the radius of turn increases as the aeroplane flies at higher airspeeds. To maintain a constant radius at higher speed the angle of bank must be increased.

steep turns and the following summary should clarify the foregoing –

(*a*) The steep turn is a developed medium turn.

(*b*) At a constant angle of bank an aeroplane will turn on a smaller radius at lower airspeeds and vice versa.

(*c*) At a particular speed, to tighten the radius of turn centripetal force (turning force) must be increased by obtaining more lift. This produces a reaction called centrifugal reaction. Because of the loading a larger angle of attack than normal is required for any particular speed.

(*d*) To overcome the extra drag caused by the larger angle of attack, more thrust is required and this means more power so that the throttle must be opened in a steep turn.

(*e*) The steeper banked the turn the greater the loading and the more power required. In a light aeroplane engine power is the limiting factor and in a sustained turn it is rarely possible to exceed a 65° angle of bank.

(*f*) The tightest turn (smallest radius) will be at the steepest bank possible for the particular aeroplane at its lowest possible speed, since for a fixed angle of bank the slower the speed the smaller the radius of turn.

(*g*) The stalling speed is higher in any turn and it increases rapidly as the angle steepens beyond 60°.

In practice a Rate 3–4 is aimed at during steep turns and the approximate angle of bank applicable to the aeroplane should be related to the horizon.

The position of the nose in relation to the horizon can be deceptive in aeroplanes with side-by-side seating because when turning to the right the pupil is sitting above the centre-line of the aircraft, the reverse being the case when turning to the left. Experience will show the pupil how the aeroplane should look in relation to the horizon under these circumstances.

Should a spiral dive develop during steep turns it may be difficult to raise the nose with the elevators. The angle of bank should be decreased when the elevators will give effective control over the fore-and-aft level of the machine in relation to the horizon. Prevention rather than cure is the secret of success

15

and any tendency for the nose to drop during the steep turn should be corrected immediately by further backward pressure on the stick. This may be considerable on some types of aircraft.

On some light aeroplanes it is difficult to high-speed stall during a steep turn, but if the manoeuvre is attempted at normal cruising power or slightly less and the radius is tightened by determined backward movement of the stick, a stall will occur. Some aircraft will 'buffet' immediately before the stall which will occur at a higher than normal speed for the reason already explained. One wing may stall before the other on certain aircraft and the usual recovery procedure should be adopted to prevent a spin developing.

A steep turn can be executed during a glide and, in the absence of power, speed must be increased above that which is usual for a gliding turn to compensate for the increased loading.

Flight Practice

COCKPIT CHECKS

a)   Trim for level flight.
b)   No insecure items in cockpit.

OUTSIDE CHECKS

Altitude: sufficient for manoeuvre.
Location: not over town or airfield, or in controlled airspace.
Position: check in relation to known landmark.

AIR EXERCISE

Steep Level Turns

a)   Look around and enter the turn in the usual manner.
b)   Allow the angle of bank to increase and, as it becomes steeper than for a medium turn, open the throttle further.
c)   Prevent the nose from dropping below the horizon by backward pressure on the stick. This will also increase the rate of turn. Maintain

15

the required angle of bank with the ailerons and balance with rudder. Keep a good lookout throughout the manoeuvre and notice the excellent downward vision because of the steep angle of bank.

d)   To resume straight flight, look out ahead and, if clear of cloud or other aircraft, roll out of the turn in the usual way using the aileron control in co-ordination with sufficient rudder to prevent skid.

e)   As the wings become level move the stick forward to keep the nose in the correct position relative to the horizon and reduce power to cruising RPM.

Steep Descending Turns

a)   From a glide increase the airspeed some 5 kt beyond that for a normal gliding turn. Check that it is clear to turn.

b)   Go into the gliding turn in the usual way but hold the aeroplane in a steeper angle of bank. Maintain the higher gliding speed with the elevators.

c)   Come out of the turn in the usual manner and return to gliding speed when the wings are level.

Stalling in the Turn (The High-speed Stall)

a)   Go into a steep turn without increasing the power.

b)   Tighten the radius of turn backward movement of the stick.

c)   Shortly before the stall buffeting may be felt. Notice the stall is at a higher speed than usual when power is on and the wings are level.

d)   To recover, ease the stick forward and increase the power. The ailerons will again become effective and capable of correcting any alteration in angle of bank caused by one wing stalling before the other.

The Spiral Dive
(to be demonstrated at a safe height)

a)   Go into a steep turn without adding power. Note the height.

b)   Allow the nose to drop below the horizon while holding on the bank.

c)   Prevent the RPM from exceeding the red line limit.

d)   Note the instrument indications –
      Rapid increase in airspeed.
      High descent rate.

15

Maximum rate of turn.
Aircraft in balance.

e) Note that the elevators are unable to raise the nose.

f) To recover –
Close the throttle.
Roll the wings level.
Ease gently out of the dive.
Open the throttle as the nose comes up to the horizon.

g) Now check the very considerable height loss.

Maximum Rate Turns

a) After making sure that it is clear to turn, apply bank smartly in the desired direction, at the same time opening the throttle fully. Control balance with rudder.

b) Steepen the angle of bank still further and increase the rate of turn by moving the stick back until just before the stall. The aeroplane is now turning at its maximum rate. Maintain a good lookout throughout the turn.

c) Roll out of the turn quickly by taking off bank in cordination with sufficient rudder to prevent skid.

d) Reduce to cruising power and move the stick forward to keep the nose in the correct position relative to the horizon as the wings become level.

16　Operation at Minimum Level

The aim of this exercise is to understand the correct flying and engine handling techniques that must be adopted when, for reasons of bad weather or special operating considerations, it is necessary to fly low.

Often the need to fly low arises from such deteriorating weather conditions as a lowering cloud base and/or poor visibility. There are, however, commercial requirements which involve low flying, typical examples being aerial photography and crop spraying. Additionally it is sometimes necessary to leave or enter a Control Zone at low level.

Low flying for its own sake is a fascinating exercise but its very attraction can be a source of considerable danger to the inexperienced pilot and the cause of annoyance to those on the ground. Because the sensation of flying near the ground is very different from that experienced normally, low flying must be considered as a separate exercise to be taught by a competent instructor before it is attempted by the pilot under training. Aspects of training peculiar to operation at minimum level may be regarded under two headings –

(*a*) Aircraft handling at low level.
(*b*) Navigation at low level.

While no minimum height is laid down for flights over open country, under para 5, Sec. 2 (General) Rules of the Air and Air Traffic Control Regulations, 1976, it is an offence to fly within 500 ft of buildings, people, etc. To prevent accidental infringement of this regulation, for all practical purposes 500 ft above ground level should be considered the minimum height to fly over unfamiliar open country. When a pilot has been forced by weather or other cause to descend below this limit, he **16** is advised to report the circumstances to the controlling authority on landing. Whatever instructions are issued by ATC it is the captain's responsibility to ensure that flight over a congested area is at sufficient height to clear the area in the event of engine failure.

So that low flying may be practised without infringing regulations approved areas are often set aside for the purpose and all exercises in this chapter are to be demonstrated in this **Low Flying Area.** Certain considerations are common to all forms of low flying and these should be understood before the various exercises are explained.

General Considerations

1. Whenever possible all cockpit checks should be completed prior to the descent so that full attention may be directed outside the aircraft once it is near the ground.

2. When the Low Flying Area includes farmland, animals must be avoided since they are usually afraid of low flying aircraft.

3. At low levels, map reading is complicated by the speed at which ground features approach and disappear from view. Low-level map reading demands a technique quite dissimilar to that used during normal cross-country flying when ground features remain in view for many minutes unless the visibility is poor.

4. High-tension cables are not easy to see and a sharp lookout must be kept for pylons and other obstacles.

5. Because of the proximity of the ground there is obviously no margin for error and since the height of the ground may vary the altimeter is of little use in determining immediate terrain clearance. For this reason it is important to learn to estimate height above the ground when flying low. Form the habit of looking at the horizon then comparing this impression with the ground just ahead of the aircraft. It is impossible to assess height above the ground by looking directly below.

6. Whereas the ground may appear quite flat when viewed from several thousand feet, every feature and undulation of the

terrain will become apparent during low flying, and the pilot must watch for ground rising at a steeper rate than the maximum climbing path of his aircraft. In bad weather avoid flying through a valley in mountainous country since this could lead to a 'blind alley'.

7. Turbulence is often associated with flight near the ground, partially because of the disturbance which results from the flow of wind over such ground features as trees, hills, ridges, buildings, etc. In summer the effect of uneven ground-heating adds to this turbulence and the effect on the aircraft is twofold –

(*a*) fluctuations in height.
(*b*) airspeed variations.

It is therefore necessary to make allowance for possible down draughts when flying over undulating ground and the hand must be kept on the throttle throughout all low flying. For the same reasons a safe airspeed must be maintained when turbulent conditions prevail.

8. The aircraft has inertia and violent changes of attitude occasioned by an evasive manoeuvre may cause an aircraft with a fairly high wing loading to 'mush' (sink) and allowance must be made when pulling up over an obstacle. In the extreme case sudden evasive action may provoke a high-speed stall. With these thoughts in mind low flying is normally practised some 500–600 ft above ground level. Tactical exercises at tree-top height are flown by Service pilots and crop spraying is performed at similar or lower levels. In each case considerable experience is required.

9. When low flying over smooth water appreciation of height often becomes difficult and level snow over featureless countryside will present the same problem. Height above water, smooth or otherwise, is difficult to judge in conditions of poor visibility and when the sun is discernible through the haze, inexperienced pilots may become disorientated.

10. Low flying will seriously affect the range of VHF radio equipment. Requests for bearings or other communications may not be clearly received unless the aircraft is relatively close to the transmitting station.

16

Importance of Accurate Flying Near the Ground

When flying near the ground, wind effect is clearly defined. Not only does drift become most apparent but the effect of the wind on ground speed can be appreciated.

The pilot's first impression during the exercise will be that of speed over the ground, the sensation becoming more apparent the lower the aircraft is flown. When flying downwind ground speed will be high and the pilot must resist the temptation to reduce power particularly when flying at 'low safe cruising speed'. Remember that airspeed keeps the aircraft flying and not ground speed.

When flying into wind the reduction in ground speed is most marked.

The effects of drift will by now be well known and allowance should be made when flying crosswind in close proximity to high obstructions. Drift during turn is the cause of certain optical illusions. When turning downwind after flying into wind, drift will create the impression that the aircraft is slipping in (Fig. 79).

Conversely when turning into a headwind after downwind flight path the aircraft will appear to skid outwards (Fig. 80). Both impressions may cause the pilot to make unnecessary and in some cases positively dangerous rudder corrections and a quick glance at the turn and slip indicator will correct any false impressions while turning with drift near the ground.

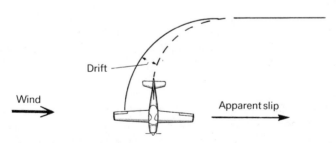

Fig. 79. Apparent slip during a turn downwind at low level.

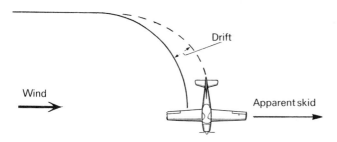

Fig. 80. Apparent skid during a turn into wind at low level.

During this part of the exercise the effects of speed, drift and the illusion of slip or skid should be noted, when the apparent inaccuracies may be checked with the instruments. Resist any tendency to make corrections which are not necessary, particularly the urge to reduce power. When flying at low level the aircraft must be correctly trimmed and while accurate flying is important this must not be at the expense of lookout.

Weather Minima

Unlike the professional pilot flying according to clearly defined company rules, the private pilot must base his decision whether or not to fly on a knowledge of his own limitations. Particularly during operation at minimum level, self-discipline is all-important.

Changes in weather can upset the best flight plan. Actual weather reports are insufficient and should be studied before the flight in conjunction with 'forecasts' for the relevant area. Avoid smoke by flying to the windward side of large towns. Particularly when looking into sun, smoke can seriously reduce low-level visibility.

When using specified entry/exit lanes to airfields within control zones the weather must be such as to allow visual contact with the ground. Before the flight all obstructions and danger/prohibited areas must be studied on an up to date map. **16**

Determining Minimum Height

(*See* 'Altimeter Settings', Vol. 4)
Regional QNH is probably the simplest altimeter setting to use during operation at minimum level since altimeter readings are then related to MSL (mean sea level) and it only remains to add 500 ft to ground level below the aircraft (or the height of obstructions to be overflown) to ensure legal en route clearance.

When joining traffic at an airfield QFE should be set on the altimeter thus relating it to airfield level. A minimum 500 ft should then be maintained around the circuit.

Preparation of Maps

All preparations relating to normal navigation apply (page 211) but during operation at minimum level prior study of the intended route and all obstructions is of special importance. Fold the map so that it is easy to handle leaving plenty of area either side of track to cater for possible deviations left or right of required track.

The Navigation Log should be prepared as for a normal cross country. When computing fuel required for the flight it should be remembered that at low levels the engine burns more gallons per hour thus reducing the range of the aircraft.

Low Flying due to Low Cloud Base

With the tendency to equip even light aircraft with comprehensive radio aids, the completion of a journey below a lowering cloud base is usually avoided in favour of flying over the cloud layer and effecting a radio let down at the destination.

On occasions when no radio facilities are available or in the event of a radio failure, low flight below cloud may be necessary. In addition to the various considerations already outlined in this chapter, there are other factors which should be understood.

16 It is important to anticipate any high ground ahead and if necessary the flight plan should be altered to re-route the aircraft over flat terrain.

Under no circumstances should cloud be entered while low flying and a height should be chosen giving the optimum ground and cloud clearance. When the visibility is normal the higher the flight the greater the range of vision ahead of the aircraft but endeavour to remain at least 200 ft below cloud.

Always fly to the right of such line features as railways when these are being followed. The feature will then remain in view from the first pilot's seat. Other aircraft which may be following the same line in the opposite direction will adopt this procedure so ensuring that both aircraft pass on opposite sides of the line feature. Be constantly on the lookout for other aircraft and be prepared for an emergency calling for extra power.

As an aid to map reading it is sometimes desirable to fly at 'low safe cruising speed' although when a reasonable amount of ceiling is available and the visibility is good normal cruising speed may be used.

Low Flying due to Bad Visibility

If because of bad visibility the pilot is forced to fly low the speed of the aircraft should be reduced to **Low Safe Cruising** and flaps should be lowered to a position slightly in excess of the maximum lift position. The advantages of this procedure are –

1. Lower stalling speed.
2. Improved rudder and elevator control as a result of the additional slipstream when power is increased to overcome the drag caused by lowering flap.
3. Smaller turning circle because of the lower speed.
4. Better forward view resulting from the nose-down attitude associated with the lowering of flap.
5. Lower cruising speed giving more time to map read under difficult conditions.

These advantages are subject to an overriding qualification in the case of both single- and multi-engined aircraft – the effect on range when power is increased. When fuel is limited it may **16** not be advisable to lower flap. Furthermore, although modern multi-engined aircraft have good 'engine out' characteristics, the lowering of flap may have an adverse effect on the single-engine performance of some earlier twins and these factors must be borne in mind.

Provided the flaps are not lowered the reductions to 'low safe cruising speed' will in many cases increase range. The opening of windows or clear vision panels will improve visibility during bad weather low flying.

Whenever low flying is occasioned by poor weather once a certain minimum has been reached, no attempt should be made to fly on into steadily deteriorating conditions, but the pilot should either (a) divert to another area where conditions are known to be better or (b) return to the home base. The point when it is decided to abandon the original flight plan will depend upon the pilot's capabilities, the terrain ahead and to some extent the type of aircraft. When the weather conditions have deteriorated to the extent that it is neither possible to divert nor turn back a Forced Landing with Power will be the only alternative (Exercise 17b).

Since low flying in poor visibility is very tiring it should, whenever possible, be avoided. When conditions make such a flight unavoidable adjust cruising height to determine the best level for visibility, always remembering not to descend below the legal limit and not to climb into controlled airspace.

Under conditions of poor visibility line features (railways, canals, motorways, etc.) are the best aid to map-reading navigation.

Low Flying in Precipitation

Rain, hail or snow will reduce visibility and in aircraft without windscreen wipers it may be necessary to open the clear vision panels provided. The effectiveness of wipers may be improved by reducing airspeed. When precipitation is of a localized nature it should be avoided by making small alterations in heading, air traffic and other considerations (such as terrain and obstacles) permitting.

Joining the Circuit

When the destination airfield is within controlled airspace access may be confined to specific Entry/Exit lanes. The horizontal and vertical extent of these lanes must be clearly understood before the flight and a good lookout must be maintained since other aircraft may be using the lane.

All instructions from ATC must be complied with and if for any reason this cannot be done, stay well clear of the circuit and notify control accordingly.

At major airports the circuit joining procedure explained on page 206 may not apply and in poor weather pilots are positioned by radar to complete the landing using one of the radio aids described in Volume 3 of this series. At this stage of training the pupil pilot will confine his low flying to **Visual Meteorological Conditions** (VMC).

Flight Practice

COCKPIT CHECKS (to be completed before the descent)

a) Fuel checked and fullest tank selected.
b) Engine controls set to make climbing power available (if applicable to type).
c) Altimeter set and DI checked.
d) Harness tight, no loose articles in cockpit and map available.

OUTSIDE CHECKS

a) Altitude: appropriate to weather and other conditions.
b) Location: in the authorized low flying area.
c) Position: check relative to a known landmark.
d) Determine wind direction.

AIR EXERCISE

Effects of Wind and Low Level Turns

Note. The following exercise is best demonstrated when there is a moderately fresh wind.

16

a)   At low safe cruising speed fly crosswind. Notice both drift and ground speed. Maintain a constant lookout for obstructions and other aircraft.

b)   Add power for all turns when flying at low safe cruising speed. Now turn into wind. Note the decrease in ground speed.

c)   Turn through 180° and as drift occurs notice that the aircraft appears to be slipping in although the turn and slip indicator is in balance. Maintain a constant height above the ground.

d)   The aircraft is now downwind and the ground speed is appreciably higher than before although the airspeed is unchanged. The temptation to compensate for higher ground speed by reducing power must be resisted.

e)   Turn upwind and as drift occurs the aircraft appears to skid outwards although the turn and slip indicator is in balance.

f)   Now become accustomed to turning in both directions at various angles of bank. Allow for drift and inertia when turning near obstacles.

Low Flying due to Low Cloud Base

a)   Imagine the cloud has lowered to 700 ft above ground level. Descend until the aircraft is well clear of cloud but remain at a safe height above the ground.

b)   If the conditions warrant, reduce to low safe cruising speed and lower flap just beyond the maximum lift position.

c)   Maintain a constant lookout for other aircraft, particularly when flying along a line feature. Be prepared to take evasive action by keeping the hand on the throttle throughout.

d)   Re-route the flight when high ground lies ahead.

Low Flying due to Bad Visibility

a)   Imagine the visibility has deteriorated. Descend until the ground below becomes clearly defined and the view ahead is improved.

b)   Reduce to low safe cruising speed and, if conditions permit, lower flap just beyond the maximum lift position. Increase power for all turns.

c)   Maintain a constant lookout for other aircraft particularly when flying along a line feature. Make full use of the clear vision panel or open windows to improve visibility. Be prepared to take evasive action by keeping the hand on the throttle throughout.

d)   Make frequent but brief reference to the instruments to confirm attitude.

16

e) Should the visibility deteriorate, abandon the flight and either divert towards better weather or return to base.

Low Flying in Precipitation

a) Fly at a height appropriate to the conditions.
b) Switch on the pitot heater and make full use of the wipers and demister (if fitted).
c) Carburettor heat as required.
d) Open the clear vision panel to improve visibility.
e) If necessary reduce airspeed to assist the wipers.
f) Make alterations in heading to avoid heavy precipitation.

Navigation at Minimum Level

(It is assumed that the usual preparations as explained on page 211 have been completed.)
a) Fly at the correct height and speed according to prevailing conditions.
b) Note the limited field of vision and that landmarks remain in view for only brief periods. Main pinpoints should be anticipated.
c) Note the limited range of radio equipment.
d) Be sure the minimum legal clearance from property is maintained and throughout the flight keep a good lookout for obstructions.
e) Make frequent checks on engine instruments and remember that at low levels the range of the aircraft will be less than normal.
f) Make early corrections to any deviation from the planned route. At low levels accurate navigation is vital.
g) Should the weather ahead deteriorate make an early decision to divert or return to base.

Circuit Joining Procedure

a) Make early contact with Air Traffic Control and remain clear of the airfield until permission to join has been obtained.
b) Keep a good lookout for other aircraft.
c) Check altimeter setting and minimum circuit height.
d) Join the circuit as instructed by ATC and report 'down-wind' and 'finals' at the appropriate time.
e) If unable to comply with *any* instruction advise the controller immediately.

16

17   Forced Landings

The sections of this chapter deal with three types of forced landing: those with power, those without power, and the special circumstances involved in ditching.

Forced Landings Without Power (Ex. 17a)

The aim of this exercise is to enable the pilot to effect a safe landing in the event of engine failure.

These days the chances of engine failure occurring in the air are remote; nevertheless the pilot must be competent to deal with the situation should it arise and take immediate action to select a suitable landing area, plan the circuit and approach and complete a successful landing.

The majority of light aircraft land at low speed and can therefore be placed in a medium-sized field with little or no risk of damage to the aircraft. Because of the low speeds involved when the correct procedure is adopted, injury to the occupants of the aircraft is extremely unlikely even when damage to the machine does occur.

By far the most common cause of forced landings without power is lack of petrol. Fuel gauges are not always as accurate as they might be, but provided the inaccuracy is understood and allowance is made when reading the instrument, there should never be any doubt about the fuel situation. In any case a visual check on fuel contents is a vital part of the pre-flight inspection. Indeed, a thorough pre-flight inspection and power check is the pilot's best insurance against a forced landing. As a double check the pilot should be fully conversant with the fuel consumption per hour and the endurance of the particular aircraft.

If circumstances are such that the pilot finds himself on a cross-country away from aerodromes and with little fuel, a **17a** **Forced Landing With Power** (Ex. 17b) should always be attempted in preference to this exercise. Without power time cannot be spent searching for a good field and once chosen the field cannot be thoroughly inspected nor the approach controlled so accurately. Furthermore in the event of a bad approach, without power it will not be possible to go round again.

In the absence of engine power height is an obvious advantage since height means time in the air and greater gliding distance. With these thoughts in mind cross-country flights should seldom be routed below 2,000 ft, preferably higher.

Imagine that while on a cross-country flight the engine fails at a height of 2,000 ft. Convert speed into distance by maintaining the level attitude of the nose then assume best gliding speed. The wind direction should be determined using smoke or, if none is visible, the take-off direction should be used. A good field should now be selected, preferably downwind.

Qualities required for an ideal forced landing field are:-

(*a*) It should be large
(*b*) Clear approaches
(*c*) It should be level
(*d*) Good surface
(*e*) Near a road and habitation so that help may be obtained after landing.

The choice of a field presents certain problems:

(*a*) While it is relatively easy to select one large enough for the landing and subsequent take-off, it is difficult to assess the surface.

(*b*) In an emergency a ploughed field can be used provided a landing is made with the furrows, although in general these should be avoided because of the soft nature of the ground.

(*c*) Colour is one indication and a large field similar in appearance to the home airfield should be sought.

(*d*) If a field can be found near a main road and habitation, so much the better for obvious reasons.

A normal circuit to the left or right should be planned, according to the aircraft's position in relation to the field and a marker point selected at the end of the downwind leg from **17**

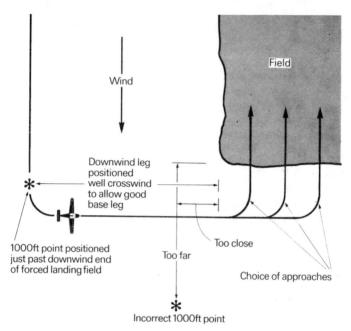

Fig. 81. Choice of approaches available to the pilot when he has chosen the correct 1,000 ft point.

which to turn on to the base leg. The marker point is the keystone of the operation and the pilot must aim to arrive over it at 1,000 ft. Incorrect selection is a common cause of misjudged forced landings and Fig. 81 shows that it should be a full **Airfield** width from the field.

Having selected a landing area and planned the circuit the pilot is now free to investigate the cause of engine failure by checking the following possibilities while gliding towards the 1,000 ft area.

(*a*) Switches: They may have been knocked 'off' accidentally.
(*b*) Fuel:Change to another tank (if fitted).
(*c*) Mechanical fuel pump failure: Switch on the electric pump.
(*d*) Carburettor icing: Operate 'hot air' control (if fitted).

17a

Referring to item (d), owing to the temperature drop in the carburettor, ice can form at temperatures above freezing in moist conditions (see Vol. 2, Chap 2 and Vol. 4, Chap 1).

If no remedial action can be taken, the normal downwind vital actions before landing should be completed but the fuel and ignition must be 'off'. When practising the exercise this part of the check is simulated, but in the case of a real engine failure both fuel and ignition must be 'off' to prevent the engine from temporarily restarting only to fail again. Such engine behaviour would be typical of fuel starvation and may prompt the pilot to climb away, only to find himself in a worse situation than before. As a precaution against fire, the mixture should be in idle cut-off. The canopy should be opened if the type permits, or the doors unlatched to assist exit, should the aircraft overturn after landing, and the harness should be tight for the same reason.

Now that a forced landing is determined, time permitting the pilot should make a distress call (Vol. 4, Chap 6).

On arrival over the 1,000 ft marker point a gliding turn on to the base leg is effected and at this stage a deliberate 'overshoot' should be planned (i.e. about one third of the way into the field). There are several reasons for this –

1. Excessive height can always be lost by using full flap or sideslipping, whereas without engine power nothing can be done to correct for insufficient height.

2. In a real forced landing the glide will be steeper without the engine firing, the propeller windmilling and causing drag.

3. If an error must occur, running into the far boundary at taxying speed is preferable to flying into the downwind hedge or fence.

While gliding on the base leg the strength of the wind can be assessed by the amount of drift away from the field. When the wind is strong the aeroplane must be prevented from drifting away from the field by turning slightly towards the boundary. Conversely, when the aircraft is obviously too high, a turn away from the field may be made. These adjustments are shown in Fig. 82. In any event the base leg must be positioned close to the boundary of the field and Fig. 81 will show how this **17a** precaution allows the pilot several alternative turning points on to the approach according to height. A base leg some distance from the field will make accurate judgement difficult.

It is, of course, possible to overshoot excessively, particularly when the wind is lighter than anticipated. When the aeroplane is so high that height must be lost before turning on to the approach, one of the following methods may be used –

1. A sideslip away from the field before turning in.

2. In extreme cases the pilot can glide past the turning point and then turn back across wind before turning in. The two methods are shown in Fig. 83.

All turns must be made towards the field. Turning away places it out of view and there is the attendant risk of under-

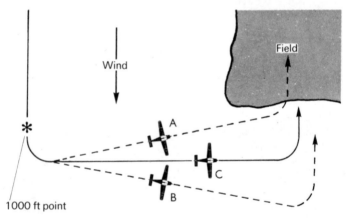

Fig. 82. Alternative method to that shown in Fig. 81 for adjusting the final approach.

shooting because of the considerable height lost in a prolonged gliding turn. Once a field has been selected the pilot should not change his mind. A change of plan during the last stages of a forced landing is rarely warranted and usually produces the wrong results.

Throughout the forced landing circuit pilots should develop a talent for assessing the aspect of the field relative to the aircraft. The ability to distinguish between too flat, too steep and the correct aspect of the chosen field will assist in guarding against gross misjudgement of the final approach.

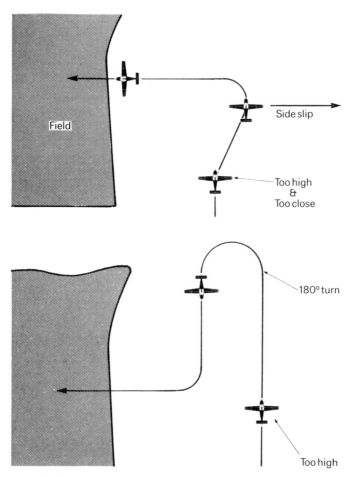

Fig. 83. Upper drawing shows another method of losing excess height before the final turn. Procedure illustrated in the lower drawing should be used only in extreme cases.

17a

When the final turn on to the approach has been made and it is certain the field can be reached, surplus height is lost by lowering full flap or, in flapless aircraft, sideslipping. A landing is then made in the usual way. When on the ground, safeguard the aircraft and notify the authorities. If possible place someone in charge of the aeroplane while the local police are notified. Tie the machine down for the night and use the safety harness to lock back the stick, thus preventing the controls from being blown about.

The foregoing explanation represents an ideal forced landing without power. There may be times when it is impossible to complete a full circuit because of the aircraft's position in relation to the selected field. In all other cases the pilot must aim to be over the marker point at 1,000 ft (above ground level) and his method of arrival will vary according to circumstances.

When practising this exercise the throttle should be opened every 500 ft or so to prevent the engine from cooling or the plugs from oiling. It is not usual to land in the practice field and power will be needed to climb away at the end of the exercise. A cold engine could turn practice into reality. In any case the throttle should be opened smoothly to prevent the engine from stalling when climbing away.

Flight Practice

For the purpose of this exercise imagine that on a cross-country flight the engine has failed at a height of 2,000 ft.

COCKPIT CHECKS

a) Throttle closed.
b) Trim for best gliding speed.

OUTSIDE CHECKS

a) Altitude: sufficient to allow 2,000 ft above ground level.
b) Location: over the authorized forced landing area.
c) Position: to be altered for each practice in relation to the forced landing field.

17a

AIR EXERCISE

a) The engine has now failed. Convert cruising speed into distance but do not allow the speed to decrease below gliding speed. Place in the gliding attitude and re-trim.

b) Determine the wind direction and select a field.

c) Turn towards the marker point which must be to one side of the downwind boundary and aim to arrive over the point at 1,000 ft. Plan as normal a circuit as possible.

d) While gliding towards the marker point try and find the cause of engine failure. Check: switches on, fuel on correct tank, electric pump on, carburettor heat 'on' under cold, damp conditions. If unable to find the cause of engine failure, carry out the pre-landing vital actions: switch off ignition and turn off the fuel (simulate) and place the mixture control in idle cut-off (simulate). Unlatch the canopy (or doors) and tighten the harness.

e) Make a distress call giving call sign, position and intentions.

f) During practice, open the throttle every 500 ft or so to keep the engine warm.

g) When over the 1,000 ft area turn on to the base leg and aim to land about one third of the way into the field. Assess the strength of the wind by the amount of drift and keep close to the downwind boundary of the field. If too low turn towards the field and if too high turn away or sideslip away from the boundary. Apply part flap as required.

h) When nearly opposite the approach turn into wind aiming to overshoot slightly. When sure of reaching the field lower full flap or sideslip off surperfluous height. Turn off the battery master switch before landing.

i) After touch-down bring the aeroplane to halt with the brakes and if necessary swing the aeroplane across wind to avoid obstacles.

j) Safeguard the aircraft and notify the home airfield and local police.

Forced Landings With Power

This exercise teaches the procedure to adopt should conditions make it necessary to terminate the flight and land in a field or on a disused airfield.

For the following reasons it may not be desirable to continue a flight –

17b

(*a*) shortage of fuel;
(*b*) approaching nightfall;
(*c*) uncertainty of position;
(*d*) bad weather.

In the event of any of these conditions, and bearing in mind that with the possible exception of (*d*) it will not be possible to return to base, a suitable field should be found and a landing made before the situation deteriorates.

Selection of a suitable field was outlined in the previous exercise and while the initial choice will be influenced by the same considerations in both the forced landing with and without power, in the former case (i.e. this exercise) the availability of power will enable the pilot to make a more detailed examination of the approaches and surface before landing.

Assuming an emergency landing has been decided upon, speed should be reduced to low safe cruising. This will vary from type to type but 60–70 kt would be suitable for most light single-engine aircraft. 15° of flap should be lowered, since this will make the aeroplane fly in a more nose-down position for any particular speed, thus improving forward visibility. By reducing speed in this way it will be possible to view the surrounding area calmly and allow more time to plan the circuit.

The wind direction can best be determined when smoke is visible, but if no indications are to be seen the direction of take-off from base can be used.

Having found a likely field a run into wind should be made over it at several hundred feet although it may be preferable to choose the longest run the field has to offer, even if this is slightly out of wind. Furthermore if there is an incline, a landing uphill even if downwind is often the best plan provided the wind is light.

During the initial run the approaches should be studied and the field should be free of ditches, high-tension cables, fences and animals. Should the weather be bad, turning points, e.g. farm buildings, ponds, etc., should be selected on which to establish a circuit. Because the aeroplane is flown at low safe **17b** cruising speed the throttle must be opened slightly while making turns, power being reduced after rolling out. In extreme cases of bad visibility the compass may be used to help maintain direction between turning points which must be selected to keep the circuit small and, where possible, the field in sight. The direction indicator may be set to zero in the landing direction. At each turning point four 90° turns can then be made on the instrument with comparative ease.

After the first circuit has been completed another approach is made, this time with a view to inspecting the surface. Like the previous run this is best made to the right of the intended landing path so that the landing area can be seen clearly by looking along the left of the aircraft. The aeroplane is lowered to near the 'hold-off' position while the ground is inspected at low speed. There should be no holes, ruts, large stones, or steep inclines. When the 'dummy run' has been completed a final circuit is made again using the turning points.

Because a good straight approach is an essential prelude to a short landing it is advisable to fly a little further downwind on this final circuit before turning on to the base leg. Speed should be reduced, flaps lowered and prior to turning on to the approach, the throttle should be opened slightly or the nose depressed. The throttle friction should be slackened (when applicable) so that power adjustments can be made with ease.

The Short Landing

On the approach the throttle should be closed almost completely while the speed is decreased to the lowest consistent with safety, so that the landing run will be as short as possible. Were the power left on while reducing speed the descent would be temporarily checked with the possibility of an overshoot. Approach speed is largely a question of experience and type of aircraft and the student pilot will obviously keep well above stalling speed. Throttle should be used to control the rate of descent and the approach path which should be a descending one when there is a hedge or fence to cross. The alternative **Creeper** approach is more or less parallel to the ground. Visibility is poor because of the nose-up attitude and for this **17b** reason too much power on the approach is to be avoided. Fig. 84 shows why this method results in a longer landing run than a descending path, particularly when there is an obstacle to cross.

During the approach the aircraft should be correctly trimmed and the airspeed checked from time to time and controlled with the elevators.

The boundary of the field should be crossed as low as possible without risking the possibility of striking it. Throttle should be decreased as the aircraft nears the ground and the descent checked by bringing back the stick in the usual way. Because of

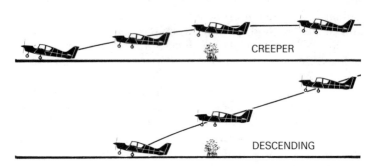

Fig. 84. Obstacle clearance on the approach.
The descending approach produces a shorter landing than the 'creeper' when an obstacle has to be crossed.

the low speed the aircraft will now be in a nose-up attitude and closing the throttle completely will cause a rapid sink. To avoid a heavy landing the throttle must not be closed until the hold-off position has been reached.

Brakes should be used to bring the aircraft to a halt and no attempt must be made to taxi until the ground ahead has been inspected on foot since an aeroplane damaged by taxying into an obstacle would be a poor end to a successful emergency landing. If the field is very small switching off the engine on touch-down will shorten the landing run and reduce damage to the propeller when running into the far hedge is unavoidable.

17b   If possible place someone in charge of the aeroplane while the local police are notified. Tie the machine down for the night and use the safety harness to lock back the stick, thus preventing the controls from being blown about.

Before attempting to fly out of the field, ensure that its surface is free from holes, soft patches etc. which could damage the undercarriage. Check the available take-off distance with the Owner's/Flight/Operating Manual.

Flight Practice

For the purpose of this exercise imagine the cloud base to be 600 ft with deteriorating visibility.

COCKPIT CHECKS

a)   Lower 15° flap (when applicable).
b)   Reduce to low safe cruising speed and re-trim.
c)   Check sufficient fuel to carry out several circuits around the selected field.

OUTSIDE CHECKS

a)   Altitude: below cloud base (in this case fly at 500 ft above ground level).
b)   Location: select suitable field with regard to wind direction and colour of surface (in Training Area).
c)   Position: downwind of selected field.

Air Exercise

(Full procedure to be demonstrated at the airfield or authorised landing ground.)
a)   Fly over the field at about 300 ft to the right of the intended landing path. Notice any high trees, overhead power cables or other obstacles which may affect the approach or climb away. At the same time judge if the field will be long enough for the landing and, when conditions permit, the take-off. Look out for fences and animals. In conditions of poor visibility use the direction indicator which may be set to zero when in the landing direction.

17b

b)   When the full length of the field has been flown, climb to circuit height – in this case 500 ft – and when level flight has been resumed find a feature on the ground which can be used as a turning point. Open the throttle slightly throughout all turns and reduce to low safe cruising power on rolling out.

c)   At the end of the crosswind leg select another ground feature and turn so a downwind leg can be flown while keeping the field in view.

d)   After the field has passed the trailing edge of the wing, select a further turning point and turn on to the base leg.

e)   Reduce speed slightly and turn on to the approach, lowering the aircraft so that it can be flown near the ground to the right of the intended landing path.

f)   Study the ground and look out for holes, ruts, large stones or steep inclines which must be avoided.

g)   When the length of the field has been flown climb away and complete another circuit using the previously selected turning points, this time flying further downwind before turning on to the base leg. Complete the vital actions.

h)   On the base leg reduce speed and lower the flaps. Slacken the throttle friction and add a little power to control the rate of descent.

i)   When nearly opposite the landing path open the throttle slightly or depress the nose for the turn on to the approach, according to the amount of height in hand.

The Short Landing

a)   When on the approach throttle back slightly, reduce to as low a speed as possible consistent with safety and open the throttle again to give steady rate of descent. Re-trim. The glide path should be a descending one adjusted with throttle. Glance at the airspeed indicator from time to time and control its reading with the elevators. Be prepared to add power should the rate of descent increase due to wind gradient near the ground. Lookout for drift and correct in the usual way.

b)   Cross low over the boundary and check the descent with elevator. The aeroplane will now be in a nose-up attitude and when near the ground the throttle should be closed, allowing it to sink to the ground.

c)   Hold the stick right back and bring the aircraft to a halt with careful use of brake. If the field is very small switch off the engine on touch-down.

17b   *d*)   Do not attempt to taxi before the ground has been examined on foot and take the necessary steps to safeguard the aeroplane. Notify the police and the home airfield.

Note: When the weather clears and the time comes to fly out of the field, the aircraft's performance, as detailed in the Owner's/Flight/Operating Manual, should be related to the take-off distance available. If there is any doubt about the ability of the aircraft to clear all obstacles with safety, the advice of an experienced pilot or flying instructor should be enlisted.

Ditching

Although ditching does not form part of the flying training syllabus in every country, a knowledge of the procedure is required, for example, by the Australian authorities*. Clearly the emergency is one to be taken seriously and therefore an outline of the factors involved is included here. Unlike most other exercises, ditching cannot be practised; nevertheless a step-by-step procedure is given under the 'Air Exercise' on page 184.

The success or otherwise of a ditching depends upon three factors:

1. Aircraft ditching characteristics.
2. Condition of the sea.
3. Strength and direction of the surface wind in relation to condition 2.

Aircraft Ditching Characteristics

The resistance of water is approximately 13 times that of air at the same speed, so that if a part of the aircraft situated some distance from its centre of gravity enters the water first considerable force will be exerted, which can seriously displace the attitude of the aircraft. For example, a fixed undercarriage will on entering the water cause a nose-down pitch. Full flap on a low-wing aircraft will have a similar effect, even if the undercarriage is retracted (when applicable to the type). Conversely, a

*Australian Exercise 14d.

17b

high-wing design, fitted with a retractable undercarriage, would enter the water fuselage first and even full flap would initially remain clear of the surface.

Experiments to determine the best airframe layout for safe ditching reveal that the ideal design would be a low- to mid-wing aircraft with a retractable undercarriage; the fuselage would plane across the water before subsiding at low speed, when the wing would offer buoyancy. However, there are few aircraft of mid-wing design and the nearest to this ideal has been found to be low-wing monoplanes with retractable undercarriages, followed by low-wing aircraft with fixed undercarriages. A high-wing aircraft with a fixed nosewheel undercarriage is known to offer the worst ditching characteristics; nevertheless there have been a number of recorded cases where such aircraft have been landed in the water without loss of life and with only minor injury.

While it has been established that the larger the aircraft the better will be its ditching qualities it should be remembered that the average light aircraft will sink within 30 seconds to two minutes according to design.

Condition of the Sea

The ever-changing sea is affected by a number of factors. Furthermore, its complex movements may bear little relationship to the prevailing surface wind. Movement of the surface is defined as follows:

Swell. This is the result of a past disturbance, possibly originating some distance away. It may be distorted by nearby land masses or other sea currents. Since it is the result of past wind effects, a heavy swell may exist in conditions of zero wind. Swell may best be understood by throwing a stone into the centre of a pond. The long ripples that reach the water's edge some appreciable time later are, in miniature form, the swell, and this movement of the surface of the sea is often referred to as the **primary swell.**

Waves. Winds in excess of 5 kt will superimpose on the primary swell a **secondary system** of waves. This assumes greater importance as the wind speed increases until, at approximately 30 kt, the wave pattern may obscure the primary swell. Whereas the primary swell may better be seen at heights of 2,000 ft or above, secondary waves are usually more recognizable below 1,000 ft. The importance of being able to determine the direction of swell will be explained under 'Choice of Landing Direction'.

Strength and Direction of the Surface Wind

Obviously smoke or steam from a nearby ship will provide an excellent indication of surface wind speed and direction. Alternatively, cloud shadows will, to a lesser degree, give similar information. In the absence of either observation the only other indication of surface wind is the appearance of the sea itself. Direction may sometimes be ascertained by looking for wind lanes (light and darker strips on the water which are best detected when looking downwind). Wind speed may be gauged as follows:

Wind Speed	*Appearance of Sea*
Light wind	Ripples of a scaly appearance.
5 kt	Very small waves.
8–10 kt	Small waves, some with foam crests.
15 kt	Larger waves with white caps.
20–28 kt	Medium size waves with long foam crests and many white caps.
30–35 kt	Larger waves with white foam blowing across the surface.
Above 35 kt	Wavecrests breaking into large streaks of foam which cover areas of the sea.

Choice of Landing Direction

Before the landing direction may be decided pilots must be able to determine:
1. Direction of primary swell.
2. Surface wind speed and direction.

This has been explained in the previous text and the choice of landing direction should be made as follows:

17

In a Calm Sea

Obviously these are the easiest conditions and the ditching should be made into wind.

In a Heavy Swell (winds up to 30kt)

Think in terms of landing in undulating sand dunes. Avoid alighting into a rising swell. When possible, alight parallel to the undulations (Fig. 85 shows the best position).

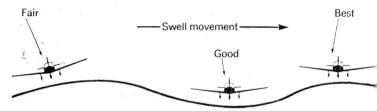

Fig. 85. Landing parallel with the swell in conditions of light to moderate wind.

When the wind is strong enough to cause pronounced drift, the aircraft must alight across the swell and towards the wind (Fig. 86).

In a Heavy Swell (winds above 35 kt)

Such winds will reduce the touchdown speed of most light aircraft to 15 kt or less, so clearly they are of prime importance while ditching. In a high wind, the swell will be shorter and the sea will be broken up into a pronounced secondary wave system, which is important. The ditching must then be made into wind and down the back of a primary swell (Fig. 87).

Positioning for the Ditching

The first consideration after alighting in the water will be speed of rescue. This is bound to be enhanced when a ship is nearby, but it is not generally realised that a ship under way will require a considerable distance to stop, typical figures being half-a-mile for a 5,000 ton steamer and up to six miles for a 200,000 ton tanker. So there is little point in ditching alongside a moving

Fig. 86. Landing across the swell and secondary waves when the wind is between 25–35 kt.

ship, while alighting well ahead of a stationary one will prolong the rescue operation.

Alighting on the Water

The aim should be to enter the water in a gentle descent and at the lowest safe speed. The best attitudes for ditching have been found to be:

1. Rectractable undercarriages, 5° to 8° nose up.
2. Fixed undercarriages, 10° to 12° nose up.

Pilots should practise assessing these aircraft attitudes, using the artificial horizon as a datum.

Deceleration will be rapid on entering the water and all occupants should protect their heads and faces, using folded **17** coats or the like. Before entering the water, all headsets and microphones should be disconnected and stowed away since these have been known to restrict exit from the aircraft. Fig. 88

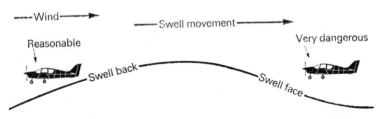

Fig. 87. Landing across the swell. Wind speeds in excess of 35 kt assume prime importance in a ditching.

illustrates some of the potentially dangerous techniques to be avoided while alighting on the water. It also shows the best method of countering drift just prior to making contact with the surface. This is very similar to a normal crosswind landing.

Abandoning the Aircraft

Much will depend on the leadership displayed by the pilot in avoiding panic. He should brief his passengers during the descent so that everyone knows what to do. The door(s) must be wedged open to ensure that it is not jammed shut on impact and, in the case of high-wing designs, that the water can enter the cabin so that the door may be opened against outside pressure. Remember that a high-wing aircraft will rapidly sink until the wing is supporting the aircraft and a wedged-open door will enable the occupants to leave the aircraft as quickly as possible. When for any reason the door will not open, a strong kick aimed at a window (preferably one that is well above water level) while lying across the seat will break the perspex and provide an alternative exit.

It is not uncommon for the windscreen to burst; notwithstanding the drama of having the sea rush in, it nevertheless

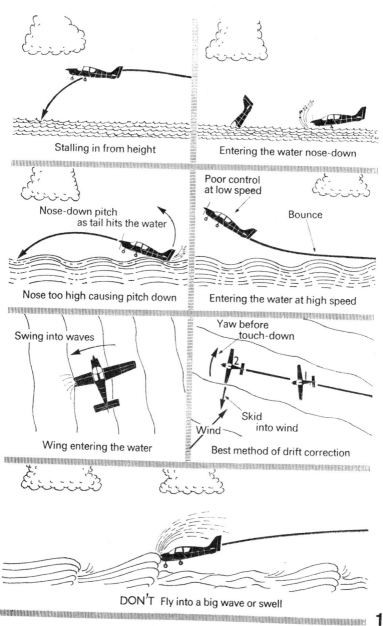

Stalling in from height

Entering the water nose-down

Nose-down pitch as tail hits the water

Poor control at low speed

Bounce

Nose too high causing pitch down

Entering the water at high speed

Swing into waves

Yaw before touch-down

Wing entering the water

Wind

Skid into wind

Best method of drift correction

DON'T Fly into a big wave or swell

17

Fig. 88. Considerations when ditching.

equalises pressure and assists with the opening of doors.

When the aircraft has come to rest in the water, release all harnesses and leave the cabin smartly – without kicking those following behind. Only after departing the aircraft should life jackets or the life raft be inflated; otherwise they will not pass through the door. Having departed the cabin, swim or paddle a safe distance away to avoid being struck by part of the sinking airframe.

AIR EXERCISE

While flying over the water the engine fails and it is necessary to alight on the water:

a)   Warn the passenger that a ditching is necessary.

b)   Put out a 'Mayday' call giving your position and intentions.

c)   If possible, plan to ditch near a ship, aiming to land ahead (if it is moving) and to one side.

d)   Determine the surface wind strength and direction and assess the direction of the swell. If the wind strength is less than 25 kt, land parallel with the swell. When the wind speed is between 25 and 35 kt, head partly into wind and across the swell but land into wind when it exceeds 35 kt.

e)   Approach at the usual gliding speed (when power is available, approach at a low speed).

f)   Remove headsets/microphones and stow them away. Get the passengers to prepare rolled coats etc. for use as protection for the head and face.

g)   In high-wing designs, open cabin windows.

h)   Check all harnesses are tight and that shoulder straps are on.

i)   Use flap as recommended (see the Owner's/Flight/Operating Manual).

j)   Near the water, open the door(s) and use a briefcase or the like to keep it/them from closing.

k)   Aim to land in a tail-down attitude on the crest of a large wave or swell. When this is not possible alight on a downslope. ON NO ACCOUNT FLY INTO THE FACE OF A SWELL.

l)   After touch-down, hold back the stick, wait for the aircraft to come to a halt, then release harnesses, open the door(s) and leave the cabin without delay.

m)   In the water, inflate the lifejackets/liferaft, keep together and move away from the aircraft.

17

n)   Make for the nearest ship, using any signalling equipment available.

18   Pilot Navigation

The aim of this exercise is to teach the student the use of maps, map reading and elementary navigational methods which will enable him to fly on a pre-determined heading to the required destination.

Navigation is a vast subject embodying techniques, some of which are beyond the capabilities of a pilot flying as the only crew member.

The motorist is confined to roads and this very limitation provides him with a ready means of finding his way from A to B. By using signposts it is possible and often practical for the motorist to cover long distances without reference to a map. Conversely the aeroplane enjoys a high degree of freedom of movement both in relation to the ground and height above it, and it is this very freedom which presents a problem. No longer guided by roads and signposts and sometimes without visual reference to the ground, the pilot must turn to navigation in one form or another if he is to find his way.

The main navigational systems are –

1. Dead Reckoning (DR).
2. Astronomical (Astro).
3. Radio and Guidance Systems.
4. Pilot Navigation.

Briefly, **Dead Reckoning Navigation** (known as DR) involves plotting the aircraft's position on special maps and charts assuming there to be no wind. These are known as **Air Positions.** At intervals, a known wind speed and direction **(Wind Velocity)** is applied to an Air Position giving a **Dead Reckoning Position.** From time to time the DR positions are confirmed by bearings on known features or radio facilities. The **18** entire flight is plotted on special navigational maps and charts which are devoid of colour and detail. These are known as **Mercator's** charts.

It will be clear that such a procedure as DR makes heavy demands on one pair of hands and a separate navigator is required to maintain the **Air Plot** as it is called. There have been epic flights in the past when pilots on their own have flown over wide stretches of water or desert while maintaining an air plot, but these are exceptional flights and the method is not suitable for the pilot who must navigate for himself.

Astronomical navigation (Astro) is based upon star observations by sextant which are referred to astronomical navigational tables. These in turn provide the necessary information to enable a navigator to transfer the star readings on to the plotting chart – an impractical task for a pilot committed to the controls of an aeroplane, and in any case, astro navigation finds its main application at night.

Radio navigation, together with **inertial guidance systems** which depend upon super-accurate gyroscopes, is a fast-developing branch of the art of navigation. The airlines of the world are largely dependent upon radio navigation and while miniaturized equipment is available for light aircraft, its function and use (explained in Volume 3) is a development which must come later in the student pilot's training, after he has mastered the method which has been evolved for the pilot-navigator. This is called **Pilot Navigation** and it represents a simple, practical way of flying from one point to another without the use of special equipment, although obviously its scope is greatly enlarged when even the simplest radio facilities are to hand.

Pilot navigation is dependent upon three fundamental requirements –

1. The ability to read a map.
2. An understanding of the effects of the wind on the aircraft's progress in relation to the ground and how to make allowance for the resultant drift, etc.
3. The accurate use of the compass, direction indicator and watch.

Maps and Charts

For convenience maps are produced on flat sheets of paper. However, the earth's surface is spherical and it is neither possible to make a flat sheet conform to the double curvature of a sphere, nor flatten a spherical surface without distortion. By depicting relatively small areas of the earth on a map these errors are minimized, but the navigator requiring a high degree of accuracy cannot be satisfied with these steps.

Various methods of projecting the earth's surface on to a flat sheet have been evolved over a great number of years. These **Projections** as they are called represent a considerable study in themselves.

Broadly speaking maps fall into two categories –

1. Topographical: used for map reading.
2. Navigational: designed for plotting in the manner described under DR navigation.

Whereas maps refer to land areas, charts depict water and here the difference ends.

So far as the Pilot-Navigator is concerned, topographical maps are the correct tool for the task since navigational sheets offer little detail for map reading and their method of projection is designed specially to meet the requirements of DR navigation.

A good topographical map should offer the following characteristics –

(*a*) Area should be accurate.
(*b*) Shape should be correct.
(*c*) A line drawn on the map should be a **Great Circle,** i.e. the shortest distance between two points on the earth's surface.

Unfortunately it is not possible to attain all of these requirements to perfection on one sheet and projections have been developed for topographical maps which represent a compromise. Whereas one projection may be ideal for a north/south country such as the British Isles, another is more suitable for an east/west country like the United States of **18**

America. Modern maps are masterpieces of design and printing, providing the pilot with a high degree of all-round accuracy.

For reference, the earth is covered by a network made up of **Meridians of Longitude** and **Parallels of Latitude** (Fig. 89).

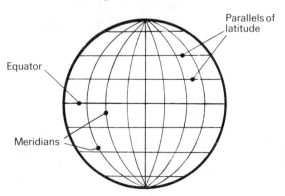

Fig. 89. Meridians and parallels.

Meridians of Longitude

The famous Greenwich meridian is designated zero, all others being referred to as east or west of Greenwich, e.g. 10° W; 45° E; 179° W, etc. On aviation maps meridians are usually shown at 10′ (minute) intervals, there being 60′ to a degree, so that a more accurate meridian can be quoted, e.g. 10° 30′ W; 45° 15′ E; 179° 59′ W, etc.

180° is where east meets west, this meridian being opposite to the Greenwich meridian on the other side of the earth. It, too, is of special interest being the **International Date Line** where, for example, it can be Monday on one side and Tuesday on the other. Fortunately domestic complications are avoided since meridian 180° passes over the Pacific Ocean until it reaches the thinly populated north-east tip of Russia.

Parallels of Latitude

The Equator is the most widely known parallel, all others being
numbered north or south of it, e.g. 57° N; 22° S; 80° N. Like

meridians these are shown at 10′ intervals on aviation maps. 90° N and 90° S are the north and south poles respectively.

Any point on the earth can be quoted by giving its **Latitude** and **Longitude** (Lat. and Long.), e.g. Kidlington Airfield is 51° 50′ N, 01° 19′ W.

The complete network made up of parallels and meridians is called a **Graticule.** In addition to providing a means of reference, the graticule is used to position the protractor when measuring direction in relation to true north, all meridians running north/south and parallels east/west.

Some maps are overprinted with an alternative graticule called the **British Modified Grid.** This is used by the Army and is unsuitable for the pilot-navigator since the Grid bears little relation to geographical N, S, E, or W. Care should be taken when purchasing maps to see that they are overprinted with latitude and longitude.

Measuring Track

Assuming it is required to fly from Le Touquet airport to Ostend airport, a line is drawn on the map joining these two points. This is called the **Required Track,** referred to in abbreviated form as Tr. Req. The bearing of the Tr. Req. is measured with a protractor position on any parallel of latitude or meridian which crosses the Track, but certain precautions must be taken. It will be remembered that the meridians converge towards the poles. This can be confirmed by measuring the distance between meridians at the foot of a topographical map and comparing the measurement with the distance between the same two at the top of the sheet. Fig. 90 shows that because of convergence towards the poles Tracks running in an easterly/westerly direction will cross each meridian at a slightly different angle. Obviously a north/south Track is not similarly affected. The protractor should therefore be positioned on the meridian or parallel which crosses nearest the centre of Track thus giving the average angle. On topographical maps such a Track represents the shortest distance between two points on the earth's surface and it is called a Great Circle.

18

Long-distance navigators prefer Tracks which cross each meridian at the same angle and these are called **Rhumb Lines.** Special maps have been produced called Mercator's Projections and all lines drawn on them are rhumb lines. These are essentially navigational projections, unsuitable for the pilot-navigator and this passing reference will suffice.

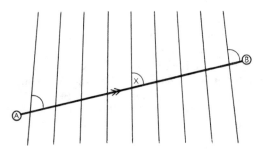

Fig. 90. Westerly/easterly track crosses each meridian at a different angle.
Compare the angle at A with that at B. By measuring the track at X the average angle will be found.

Scale

A map is, in fact, a scale drawing of a particular area of the earth. Those found in a school atlas are produced to show a large area on a relatively small sheet and a scale of 100 miles or more to the inch is common. At the other extreme are the maps used by surveyors and sometimes hikers, which indicate a mile for every $2\frac{1}{2}$ in on the sheet. Such maps are very detailed, showing quite small buildings and every minor bend in a country lane. Aviation requirements fall between these two examples and those in common use are –

(*a*) The 1:250,000 series.
(*b*) The 1:500,000 series.
(*c*) The 1:1,000,000 series.

They are usually referred to as the 'quarter-million', 'half-million', or 'million series' respectively. As the terms imply, one unit on, for example, a half-million map denotes 500,000 units on the earth. For practical purposes this amounts to eight statute miles to the inch but an accurate scale is printed on the map. Distances may be measured in statute miles, nautical miles or kilometres and navigational rules are obtainable, calibrated in all three units. It is international practice to talk in terms of nautical miles.

Whereas speed is measured in miles per hour when dealing in statute miles, 100 nautical miles covered in one hour is referred to as 100 knots. The merits and demerits of the two systems need not be gone into here, but it is convenient to work in whichever units are marked on the aircraft's airspeed indicator, although there is a tendency to standardize the calibration of these instruments in knots.

Converting Nautical Miles, Statute Miles and Kilometres

A statute mile contains 5,280 ft, whereas a nautical mile measures 6,080 ft. The nautical mile represents an attempt to relate a measuring unit to the dimensions of the earth and it is described as 'the average length of one minute of arc'. It may be necessary to convert kilometres to statute miles or statute miles to nautical miles. Most navigational computers are able to make these conversions (described in Chapter 5, Vol. 4), but in the absence of a computer the following figure are worth remembering –

$$33 \text{ n.m.} = 38 \text{ st.m.} = 61 \text{ km.}$$

Thus to convert 120 n.m. to st.m. the answer is

$$\frac{120}{33} \times \frac{38}{1} = 138 \text{ st.m.}$$

or 250 st.m. converted to n.m. is

$$\frac{250}{38} \times \frac{33}{1} = 217 \text{ n.m.}$$

18

Relief

Although high ground is not always of value as a map-reading feature, a prominent hill or mountain can present an excellent pinpoint. Furthermore changes in depth when flying over water can often be seen quite clearly. In addition, high ground presents a hazard in conditions of poor visibility, low cloud and darkness. For all of these reasons, relief is of interest to the pilot-navigator and the various means of showing it on a map are listed below –

1. Spot heights (and depths).
2. Layer tints.
3. Contours.
4. Form lines.
5. Hill shading.
6. Hachures.

1. *Spot Heights* indicate the higher points, usually of a prominent nature, which have been measured above **Mean Sea Level (MSL).** On the quarter-million series, heights are quoted in feet while metres are used on some half-million maps. A conversion table from metres to feet is printed in the margin on these sheets and care should be taken not to use incorrect units when reading heights or depths.

2. *Layer Tints are used in conjunction with contour lines of* topographical maps. The palest shades refer to the lower regions, white being reserved for ground at sea level. The tints become darker as higher ground is indicated and a chart showing heights against each shade is printed on the margin of the map.

3. *Contours* are lines joining all places of equal height. With practice they give a good indication of the shape of a hill or mountain. Widely spread, they denote a gentle rise or fall, whereas a steep-sided mountain will be depicted as a series of closely spaced contour lines. At convenient intervals the lines are broken and the height for that particular contour is printed in the resultant space.

18   4. *Form Lines* are similar to contours except that they are an approximation in the form of concentric rings rather than the accurate picture of rising ground presented by contour lines.

5. *Hill Shading* is not in general use on aviation maps these days, partly because it tends to obliterate other details. It represents an attempt to endow the map with a three-dimensional effect, by shading those portions of the high ground which would lie in the shadows when the sun is in a certain position.

6. *Hachures* are not to be found on topographical maps. In this method the approximate outline of a range of hills is shown as a row of short, fence-like lines. Hachures may be seen on navigational plotting sheets and their purpose is to indicate the presence of high ground rather than attempt to describe it.

The pilot-navigator need only concern himself with those methods which are common to topographical maps, namely spot heights, layer tints and contour lines. A combination of all three is usual.

Conventional Signs

Features on the map such as airfields, railways, roads, woods and even tunnels and power lines are depicted by the use of pictorial representations known as **Conventional Signs.**

Most maps list these symbols either in the margin or on the back of the sheet and the pilot-navigator is advised to become conversant with them at an early stage in his cross-country flying. These signs vary slightly from one series of maps to another but many are common to both.

Airspeed Corrections

The airspeed indicator is a pressure instrument, dependent upon the force exerted by air at speed for its readings. Should the density of the air be affected by temperature or height, the airspeed indicator will fail to give a true speed. Furthermore, while every endeavour is made to install the instrument away from airflow disturbances, errors caused by its positioning do occur, in addition to inaccuracies in the instrument itself.

18

Therefore three separate airspeeds exist and these are listed below –

Name	Abbreviation	Description
Indicated airspeed	IAS	The actual speed indicated on the airspeed indicator.
Rectified airspeed	RAS	This is indicated airspeed corrected for position and instrument error.
True airspeed	TAS	This is rectified airspeed corrected for height and temperature and it represents the actual speed of the aeroplane in relation to the surrounding air.

The correction from IAS to RAS is effected by a correction card which will be adjacent to the airspeed indicator unless the errors are so small that it is deemed unnecessary to have one. RAS is converted to TAS on the navigational computer by setting the height against the outside air temperature, when the equivalent TAS can be read off against any RAS (*see* Chapter 5, Vol. 4). In so far as navigational problems are concerned, all workings must be in TAS. At the height at which most light aeroplane flying occurs, the difference between RAS and TAS will vary by 10 kt or so, 5 kt being typical. Conversely a jet aircraft flying at 40,000 ft at a TAS of 500 kt may only indicate 255 kt.

Map Reading

By now the student should be able to draw the required track, express its bearing in relation to true north and measure the distance between the points of departure and arrival. Features along the Track should be studied, particular attention being paid to railways which cross its path. Except in industrial areas where a maze of railway lines exist, they are, together with coast lines and rivers perhaps the most useful features as an aid to map reading, with rivers, canals and lakes a close second. Roads may be confusing from the air; with the exception of motorways, main and secondary roads look very similar. Generally roads should be used as a means of confirmation and Fig. 91 is an example. This shows a railway which crosses the Track near a road-rail crossing. Should the aeroplane cross the road before the railway it is clearly to starboard of Track.

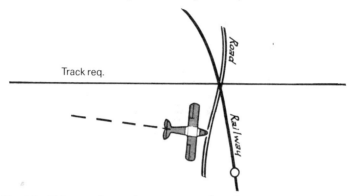

Fig. 91. The use of a road as a means of confirmation in conjunction with a railway line.

Woods are useful although subject to change due to forestry activity and because of this care should be taken. Airfields can be confusing by virtue of their close proximity to one another in certain areas. East Anglia is a particular example, there being an airfield every few miles. Here again these can be used to confirm a position and Fig. 92 shows two similar villages on a main road, one with a nearby airfield and in this case the pilot is approaching Barmby-on-the-Moor.

While hills and mountains can be a further aid, it should be remembered that what appears to be a hill of some magnitude from the ground can look featureless from a height of 2,000 ft or more.

Having studied the Track and the features over which it passes, the more prominent ones should be anticipated during the flight. So as to draw attention to these features, some pilots

18

like to ring them before flight. It is neither necessary nor desirable to map-read every yard of the countryside; rather the aim should be to fly an accurate heading from one feature of importance to another. These features are called **Pinpoints** and it is as well to fly a little to starboard of Track so that they can be seen when looking from the left of the aircraft. An aeroplane dead on Track will obscure the pilot's view of these pinpoints.

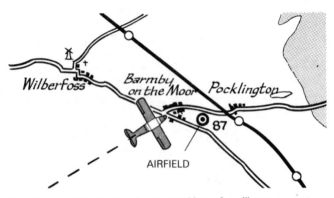

Fig. 92. An airfield aids the recognition of a village.

These remarks are not meant to imply that no regard should be paid to those features which pass on the other side, but unless the seating is arranged tandem fashion, i.e. Chipmunk, Piper Cub, etc., more can be seen looking out of the left from the first pilot's seat. Throughout the flight the map should be held so that the Track coincides with the direction of flight. In this way features on the map will appear in the same position relative to the pilot as those on the ground. Such a procedure is called **Orientation.** The map should be neatly folded to a size easily handled in the aeroplane, with the Track running down the centre.

The Triangle of Velocities

Navigation would be simple in a world free of winds. Having measured the Track, the pilot could set this heading on the compass after correcting it for variation and deviation (page 87) and provided the aircraft was steered accurately all would be well. However, wind is a feature of this world and it has a profound effect on aerial navigation. Wind is movement of a mass of air in relation to the ground. The aeroplane being supported in an air mass is susceptible to its movements like a goldfish carried in its tank from one room to another. The water is moved and the fish goes with it.

Put into more specific terms, an aeroplane cruising at 100 kt TAS from Detroit Metro to a point 100 n.m. due east would in still air arrive over that point after 60 min. The same flight against a 20 kt wind would reduce the speed over the ground to 80 kt although the airspeed would remain unaltered. The flight would now have an elapsed time of 75 min, i.e. 100 n.m. at 80 kt.

Now consider the flight with a 20 kt tailwind. Speed over the ground would be 120 kt and a flight of 100 n.m. distance would take only 50 min. Fig. 93 illustrates the effect of a 20 kt

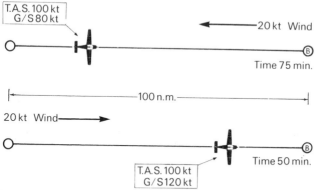

Fig. 93. The effect of headwind and tailwind on ground speed and time of flight.

headwind and tailwind and it will be apparent that in these cases, provided the Track of 090° is corrected for variation and deviation, then accurately steered as a heading, the aeroplane will arrive over point B.

18

The situation becomes a little more complex when the wind is at an angle to the Track. Taking the same flight as an example with a 20 kt wind from the north, speed over the ground would be little affected, but if 090° is steered at the end of 60 min flying the aeroplane would be 20 n.m. south of Track. To arrive over B it is necessary to aim at an imaginary position 20 n.m. north of it thus compensating for the drift caused by the wind (Fig. 94). From this explanation the importance of the wind can

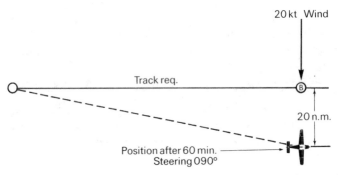

Fig. 94. The wind effect after 60 minutes flying with a 90° crosswind.

be seen, together with the necessity of allowing for its effect in order to make good the required Track. Wind strength as well as its direction will affect the aeroplane and the combined factors of wind speed and direction are known as a **Wind Velocity.** Prior to a cross-country flight this can be obtained from the meteorological office or airfield control. It is expressed as a direction and speed, e.g. 045°/25 kt, or 215°/15 MPH. The direction refers to origin of the wind and not its line of travel. The first example means that the wind is blowing *from* 045° at 25 kt. Knots are usually quoted rather than MPH.

Because the wind strength and direction tend to alter with height, a weather report will include wind velocities at different levels and that quoted nearest to the desired cruising height should be used.

With a wind velocity in his possession, the TAS of his aeroplane decided and the Tr. Req. drawn and measured for length and bearing, the pilot is now able to calculate the missing links which are –

1. The true heading (when corrected for variation and deviation; this is steered to compensate for the wind).
2. The ground speed.
3. The elapsed time for the flight.

The Airtour Computer is one of several navigational computers capable of solving such a problem rapidly, but before using these tools of navigation (explained in Vol. 4) it is imperative that the student pilot should understand the theory of the **Triangle of Velocities.**

Taking the simple case quoted of a Tr. Req. 090°, TAS 100 kt and a wind velocity (W/V) of 360°/20 kt, it is possible to draw the various speeds and directions (velocities) in relation to one another, using a protractor and a pair of dividers or compasses. Squared paper is preferable but plain will suffice and the following sequence should be followed –

1. Draw the Tr. Req. in the direction 090° but pay no attention to its length at this stage. The conventional sign for Track is ➤➤ and it should be marked accordingly to distinguish it from other lines to be drawn later.
2. At the destination end of the Track, draw a line to represent the wind direction. Remember this is quoted *from* its origin and in consequence will always blow towards the Track. The wind direction should be marked ➤➤➤ which is the conventional sign for a W/V. The wind direction and track have now been drawn in relation to one another.
3. Next insert the wind speed. Any scale can be used for this purpose; millimetres will be found convenient. The wind speed in this case is 20 kt, so that 20 mm should be set on the dividers and transferred to the wind direction line, thus completing the wind velocity.
4. The TAS is 100 kt, so that 100 mm should be set on the dividers. Place one leg on the wind velocity and the other on the Track; by joining these two points the triangle of velocities is completed and this is shown in Fig. 95. The last side is the true

18

heading (Hdg. T.) and it is marked →—. The Hdg. T. is measured using a protractor at the end of the triangle opposite to the wind velocity.

5. Using the dividers in conjunction with the millimetre scale on a rule, measure the length of the Track line to obtain the

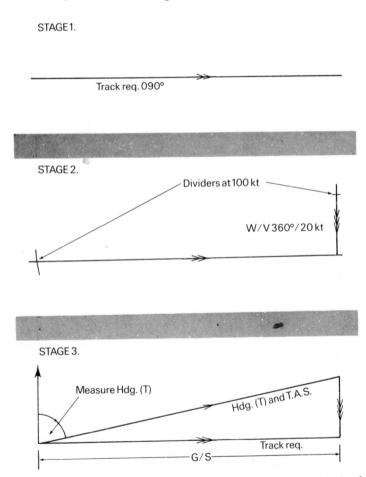

STAGE 1.

Track req. 090°

STAGE 2.

Dividers at 100 kt

W/V 360°/20 kt

STAGE 3.

Measure Hdg. (T)

Hdg. (T) and T.A.S.

Track req.

G/S

Fig. 95. Squared paper will assist in the construction of the triangle of velocities.

ground speed (G/S). This process is effected in a matter of seconds with a navigational computer – an essential item for the pilot-navigator.

Corrections in Flight

It is often said that, if the aircraft remains on Track during the first ten minutes or so of a cross-country, there should be little difficulty during the remainder of the flight. When the pilot has determined the heading to steer correctly and then proceeded to fly accurately on that heading, the aeroplane is bound to follow the required track unless the wind velocity obtained before the flight is at fault. This can happen and it is essential to correct any errors during the early stages of the flight.

Initially a climb to cruising altitude is made and with the airspeed settled the aeroplane is positioned on heading so that the airfield appears under the left window. The pilot has now **Set Heading** and a note to this effect should be made on the **Flight Log** (which is described later), using the abbreviation S/H and noting the time. To this should be added the elapsed time for the flight, thus obtaining an arrival time at destination. This is called the **Estimated Time of Arrival** (ETA).

Within the first five or ten minutes a good pinpoint should be found, so determining the exact position of the aircraft relative to the Tr. Req. Should the aeroplane be to one side of Track a correction will have to be made since the error will more than likely increase progressively during the flight unless there is a change in windspeed or direction (or both).

The actual path of the aircraft over the ground is called the **Track Made Good (TMG).** The angular difference between the TMG and the Tr. Req. as drawn on the map is called the **Track Error.** This must be known before a suitable alteration of heading can be made.

By drawing short lines fanning out either side of Track at 5° intervals (known as **Fan Lines**), a simple but effective means of estimating track error is available to the pilot in the early stages of training. This is shown in Fig. 96 and were the pilot to find himself over the small lake marked 'Res.' the track error would **18** be 9° S. (Starboard). An alteration of heading by 9° P. (Port) will cause the aeroplane to fly more or less parallel to Track, and the usual procedure is to double the track error and alter heading, in this case 18° P. The new heading should be steered for the same time as was flown on the original heading before the alteration was made, when the aeroplane will be back on

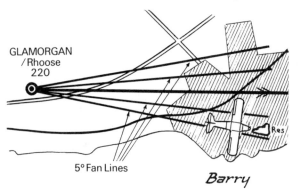

GLAMORGAN
/Rhoose
220

5° Fan Lines

Barry

Fig. 96. The use of 5° fan lines.
For determining track error during the early stages of a cross-country flight.

Track. An alteration of 9° S. will maintain Track unless there is a further change in the wind. By this procedure the aeroplane is made to follow Track during the early stages of the flight, and the addition of 5° lines at the destination will help the pilot to make corrections in the final stages of the cross-country should he find himself off Track. The use of 5° lines is recommended as an early training aid.

The One-in-Sixty Rule

The wind velocity may change during a cross-country. While variations in windspeed and/or direction are usually quite small during flights of 100 n.m. or so, there can be a considerable alteration when flying from coastal regions to points inland, or vice versa.

The primary method of estimating track error, and computing an alteration of heading to reach destination, is known as the **One-in-Sixty Rule.** This technique is ideally suited to pilot navigation and is based on the fact that at a distance of 60 miles, an aeroplane is approximately one degree off Track if it is one mile to one side of the intended position. To give other examples: one mile off Track after 30 miles flying = 2° track error; 3 miles off Track after 90 miles flying = 2° track error. The proportion is 1 in 60 throughout and any units can be used, statute miles, nautical miles or kilometres. Suppose the pilot noted the aircraft to be 4 n.m. off Track after flying for 40 n.m., the track error would be $\frac{4}{40} \times 60 = 6°$

This rule has various applications and all are intended to be calculated mentally during flight. Imagine the situation which is illustrated in Fig. 97. The pilot finds himself 3 n.m. to Port of

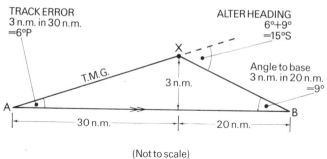

(Not to scale)

Fig. 97. Application of the one-in-sixty rule.

Track after 30 n.m. flying, with a further 20 n.m. to fly. What heading should he steer to arrive over his destination? By using the 1-in-60 rule the number of degrees to alter heading is easily calculated.

Three n.m. to Port after 30 n.m. flying is a track error of 6° P. An alteration of 6° S. will make the aeroplane fly more or less parallel to Track but 3 n.m. to one side of it. Three nautical miles to Port with a further 20 n.m. to go amounts to a 9° correction, assuming the aeroplane to be flying parallel to **18**

Track. The first calculation is the track error from base and the second represents the track error to destination. By combining the two results, an alteration of heading to reach destination is obtained – in this case 6°+9° = 15° to Starboard.

These corrections make no allowance for the changing relationship between the aircraft's heading and the W/V but the results are sufficiently accurate for practical purposes.

Time

Map reading can be assisted by marking positions along the Track at 5- or 10-minute intervals. The distance between these marks on the map will depend upon the ground speed which has been found on the computer before flight.

Some pilots prefer to divide the Track into four equal parts and calculate the elapsed time to each mark on the map. At the half-way mark, the **Estimated Time of Arrival (ETA)** can be up-dated by doubling the time of flight up to that point.

The Flight Plan

Before embarking on a cross-country flight the student pilot will be required to make a **Flight Plan** (Fig. 98) and, at some major airports, details from this will be required by Air Traffic Control.

Before planning the flight, certain information such as danger and prohibited areas, safety heights according to the terrain *en route*, etc., can be ascertained from the briefing room. A weather report or, more correctly, a **Route Forecast** will be obtained from the Meteorological Office and this will include the wind velocity at various flight levels.

Printed flight plan forms are available and the procedure is to enter all known factors, i.e. W/V, Tr. Req., TAS altitude or level of flight, variation, distance and then compute true heading, magnetic heading, ground speed, and time of flight. Other important information will include fuel contents, endurance, sector safe altitudes on each leg of the flight and the radio frequencies likely to be used en route. If weather deteriorates it may be necessary to land at another airfield and these alternative airfields must be selected at this stage.

18

FLIGHT PLAN

Pilot **A. PENZER**		A/C **G–ABCD**	Date	ETD **11/10**

Route Clearance	Checked by
RHOOSE – STAVERTON – ELMDON (LAND)	
ELMDON – RHOOSE	*ebott*
VAR: Alternate **COVENTRY – BRISTOL LULSGATE**	

Fuel Carried **17 Gall**	Consumption **5/hr**	Range **255 NM**	Endurance **3 Hrs**

Alt.	W/V	Temp °C.	IAS	QNH	Facility	Freq.	Facility	Freq.
2000'	120/20	+11°	83K	1008	STAVERTON TWR	122·9	BRISTOL HOMER	127·25
4000'	130/25	+7°	81K	1010	STAVERTON RADAR	125·65	BRECON VOR	116·3
					B'HAM APP.	120·5	RHOOSE NDB	363·5
					COVENTRY TWR	119·25		

From	To	Min. Alt.	Flt. Level	Tr. (T)	TAS	Hdg. (M)	G/S	Dist.	Time	Fuel
CARDIFF/ RHOOSE	STAVERTON	1500		055°	85K	076°	75K	NM 53	42½	3½
STAVERTON	B'HAM/ ELMDON	3000		025°	85K	048°	85K	37	26	2¼
B'HAM/ ELMDON	CARDIFF/ RHOOSE	2000		223°	85K	214°	81K	87	64½	5½

FLIGHT LOG — TOTALS:-

Time	Position	Observations / Messages	Hdg. (C)	New G/S	ETA	Fuel Left
11.15	AIRBORNE	Climb to 3500'	076°	75K	12·02½	
11.20	S/H STAVERTON					
11.45	RIVER WYE	TMG 057° A/H 4°P	072°	76K	12·02	
12.02	STAVERTON	S/H ELMDON	050°	85K	12·28	13½
12·12½	RAIL/RIVER	Cross on Track				
12.29	ELMDON	Descending. Landed 12.38				
13.55	AIRBORNE	Climb to 3500'				
14.05	S/H RHOOSE		215°	81K	15.09½	
14.38	ROSS 2NM STBD. T.E. 3°P A/H 6°S		221°	"	"	
14.51½	USK 1NM STBD.					6½
15.10	RHOOSE	Descending. Landed 15.15				

SIGNATURE: **A. Penzer**

18

Fig. 98. Typical Flight Plan/Flight Log.

To avoid serious mistakes, it is good practice to estimate Tr. Req., distance, drift and time of flight before using the computer. With practice good approximations can be made and these will safeguard against such fundamental mistakes as applying the wind in the wrong direction on the computer, to mention but one possibility.

The second portion of the form is usually devoted to the **Flight Log.** This is for 'in flight' information and the pilot is well advised to prepare a skeleton log before take-off. It is difficult to write while flying and the various pinpoints expected during the flight can be listed, leaving only the times and heading alterations to be noted. During flight, information is logged in the following order –

QFE and QNH ('The Altimeter', Chapter 4, Vol. 4)
Time S/H and first ETA.
Time at pinpoints.
Alterations of heading (A/H) and time.
Amended ETA.
Time of arrival over destination.
Regular fuel checks should also be noted.

The specimen flight plan shown in Fig. 98 is one of several types which may be held on a convenient knee board.

Joining the Circuit

On arrival at the airfield of destination it will be necessary to have the following information –

1. Airfield height.
2. Direction of circuit (left or right).
3. Circuit Height.
4. Runway in use or landing direction.
5. Wind speed and direction.
6. Other traffic on the circuit or approaching the field.
7. QNH/QFE.

18   The first item will be printed on the map next to the airfield symbol. All the other information together with a barometric setting for the altimeter is usually passed over the radio. When none is available numbers 2 and 4 can be seen by referring to the signals area and the relevant signals are to be found on page 228. Wind direction and its speed can be assessed by the appearance of the wind sock, and the pilot must maintain a careful watch for other traffic.

In the absence of specific instructions from control, towards the latter stages of the cross-country a gradual descent should begin while maintaining the TAS, until the aeroplane is at 2,000 ft. It will then be possible to fly over the airfield on arrival and study the Signals Area without interrupting other aircraft flying below at circuit height.

While lowering to circuit height steps must be taken to avoid descending on to aircraft already on the circuit. A curved descent should be made on the **Dead Side** of the airfield, i.e. the opposite side to that around which the circuit is being flown. Flying will be in the direction of the circuit in force. At circuit height (usually 800–1,000 ft) it is essential to turn across wind as soon as the aeroplane is abreast of the up-wind end of the runway, when a normal circuit can then be completed. By keeping close to the end of the runway there will be no danger of collision with aircraft taking off since they will not have reached circuit height at that point.

For non-radio aircraft, or at airfields without radio service a 'Green' (lamp signal) will be given from Control when on the approach, but some airfields operate on 'negative signals'. This means that the pilot is free to land unless he receives a 'Red' when he must immediately go round again.

Action to be Taken when Lost

On the basis that prevention is always better than cure, it is as well to understand those factors most likely to save the pilot from becoming lost. While an accurately prepared flight plan is a sound basis for a cross-country flight, good map reading is all important. An incorrect heading will not lose the accurate map reader. He must learn to select the good pinpoint from the **18** worthless and develop the ability to find his way back on Track when the wind differs from that forecasted for the flight.

By reading from map to ground there will be little danger of becoming confused while trying to make a feature on the ground fit the map. It is not possible to present every detail on a quarter-million sheet and even less detail is available on the half million series, so that only those features which appear on the map should be used.

Following in importance is the ability to steer accurately. There is little point in calculating a heading to steer with precision only to ignore it in the air. The direction indicator should be re-set every 10 to 15 minutes because of **Precession,** i.e. its tendency to wander out of alignment with the compass. Care should be taken when synchronizing the instrument that the compass is reading accurately and not subject to the various errors described on page 85. It is not unknown to set the DI only to leave the setting knob in the 'caged' position so that no changes of heading are indicated. When a compass is the only means of steering a course, its behaviour as explained on page 90 should be fully understood.

It is an established fact that during his early cross-country flights the student readily loses his appreciation of time between features, particularly when for one reason or another he misses an expected pinpoint. Alternatively he may expect a pinpoint to appear when it is not in fact due for three or four minutes. In his anxiety to see the pinpoint before time he fails to maintain the correct heading and strays off Track. Soon confidence is lost and thinking becomes confused with the attendant effect on his sense of time.

Time marks (page 204) are a great help but perhaps the best insurance against the situation outlined in the previous paragraph is a well-kept flight log. When uncertain of position the log is of real assistance since it gives the time over the last pinpoint which was recognized with certainty, and this provides a basis for re-assessment.

Unless a major blunder has occurred the aeroplane is unlikely to be farther from its correct position than a distance equivalent to 10 per cent of the mileage flown. This means that after flying 100 n.m. the aircraft will be within a radius of 10 n.m. from the intended position when lost, and *pro rata*. This is called a **Circle of Uncertainty** and its use confines the search area when lost to a proportion which is related to the length of the flight. The longer the time in the air since the last position of certainty, the greater the possible error and therefore the larger the circle of uncertainty.

When lost the following procedure should be adopted –

1. Log the time when 'Lost Procedure' is commenced. Check sector safe altitude.

2. Check the fuel content and if there is little remaining prepare for a forced landing with power (Exercise 17b).

3. Check the compass reading and when applicable ensure the DI is correctly synchronized and functioning properly.

4. Do not wander about aimlessly but hold the pre-arranged heading, height and airspeed.

5. Establish a circle of uncertainty by drawing a free-hand circle on the map around the present DR position which can be estimated from the time marks. The radius of the circle will be approximately one-tenth of the distance flown since the last pinpoint which was recognized with certainty.

6. Reverse the normal procedure by reading from ground to map, paying particular attention to important features which are bound to be shown on the map while looking out for prominent landmarks within the circle of uncertainty. The features may not be recognized immediately but they should be logged together with the time so that a chain of good pinpoints is built up, e.g. 11.05 large town, 11.12 river, 11.15 main railway, etc. In this way a picture can be built up which will fit within the framework of the circle of uncertainty.

When the aircraft is known to be more or less on Track but the destination fails to appear on time, the flight plan should be adhered to and the heading continued after ETA for a further 10 per cent of the calculated flight time. This is in accordance with the circle of uncertainty procedure.

It is possible that the circle of uncertainty may cover feature-less country, when an alternative procedure is preferable. This **18** makes use of a prominent feature which is known to be on one side of the aircraft or possibly ahead of it. A **Line Feature** (railway, river or canal, coastline, motorway, etc.) should be chosen so that a heading alteration can be made in the certain knowledge that it is bound to be crossed at one point or another. A localized pinpoint such as a town or an airfield is too easily missed when lost. To quote an example, imagine a flight from Exeter airfield to Southampton Eastleigh. Midway the pilot becomes lost and decides to use the line feature method of establishing his position after going through items 1–4. In this case he knows that the south coast is on his starboard side although it is out of sight. By turning south he is bound to reach it although the point of interception will probably be unknown. Over the coast he should turn left and log features as they are passed together with the time and the heading of the coastline, until a series of landmarks has presented a picture which will enable him to relate his position with the map.

On some occasions it may be known that the aeroplane is somewhere in an area bounded by two converging railway lines which eventually meet in a large town. These line features will 'funnel' the pilot towards the town and it will merely be necessary to fly on while looking for a railway which is converging with the path of the aircraft. By following this railway and looking out for the other line as a confirmation, the pilot will be guided towards the town and a new heading to destination can then be estimated.

Finally the pilot who is lost should realize that, provided he has plenty of fuel and daylight, an airfield is bound to appear sooner or later in most parts of the country, even if it is disused, and a skilful forced landing with power makes any good-sized field an airfield for a light aeroplane.

While early pilot navigation exercises should be confined to map reading without the use of radio navaids, a pilot who becomes lost should not hesitate to enlist the help of the Air Traffic Control Service. It is there to assist.

Flight Practice

Preparation before Flight

Note: It is assumed that the aircraft documents (C of A, C of R, insurance, maintenance release etc.) have been checked and found to be in order and that the aircraft is fuelled and within its weight and balance limits.

a) Study danger and prohibited areas and arrange to fly around them. Determine the minimum safe height in relation to high ground. Radio facilities and frequencies *en route* are usually obtained at this stage.

b) Obtain a route forecast and a wind velocity applicable to the height(s) intended during the cross-country.

c) Draw the required track on the map together with 5° fan lines at each end. Estimate the track, distance, drift and time of flight and note on a separate sheet of paper for comparison with the calculated results later. Measure the track and enter its bearing and distance on the flight plan together with the following information: W/V, height, TAS, variation and any other details called for on the printed form.

d) Compute Hdg.T and G/S and add this information to the flight plan. Calculate the time of flight and using the relevant variation convert Hdg.T to Hdg.M. Repeat this procedure for each leg of the flight when the cross-country involves more than one. Fold the map(s) to a convenient size.

e) Study the track and either indicate time marks at 5- or 10-minute intervals or divide it into four equal parts. Ring important pinpoints and on the basis of the calculated G/S note the elapsed time to each of these. At this stage, select alternative airfields for use in the event of enforced changes of plan (weather, fuel shortage etc.).

f) With the completed flight plan book out.

g) On joining the aircraft ensure that there is ample fuel for the flight.

h) Carry out a thorough preflight inspection of the aircraft checking fuel contents, Rotating Beacon, pitot heat and presence of first aid kit and serviceable fire extinguisher.

i) Convert Hdg.M to Hdg.C by referring to deviation card.

(The difference between TAS and IAS can usually be ignored on light aircraft at heights in the region of 2,000 ft, but at greater altitudes and high temperatures it must be taken into account.)

j) Set the altimeter to the QNH (to be obtained from Airfield Control over the R/T).

18

AIR EXERCISE

a)   Climb to the pre-determined cruising altitude and so manoeuvre the aircraft that it passes slightly to the right of the airfield when on heading. Log the time S/H and by adding the calculated time of flight note the ETA.

b)   Steer the heading accurately and after 5 to 10 minutes flying, look for a good pinpoint. If this is on Track proceed with the pre-arranged heading; if not determine the track error by using the 5° Fan lines. Log the time over the pinpoint and note the elapsed time for use during the correction. Double the track error and A/H (alter Heading) by that amount towards track. When track has been regained, halve the alteration of heading so that the aeroplane maintains the required track. In the absence of a good pinpoint track will be regained after flying the first correction for the number of minutes taken to reach the position which was off track.

c)   Check the DI with the compass every 10–15 minutes and reset whenever necessary.

d)   Do not map read all the time but concentrate on steering an accurate heading between the pre-selected pinpoints.

e)   Maintain the log by noting the time at each pinpoint. Log any alterations of heading.

f)   At the half-way mark check the time and if necessary revise the ETA.

g)   In the absence of advice from control, when nearing destination, provided there is no high ground, reduce power and descend to 2,000 ft while maintaining the airspeed constant.

h)   Obtain landing instructions or when there is no radio fly over the signals area and check –

    1. Landing direction.
    2. Direction of circuit.
    3. Obstruction or special signals.

On the 'dead side' of the airfield descend on a curved path to circuit height keep a good lookout for other traffic. Ascertain the airfield height from the map and level out at 800 or 1,000 ft above it according to local rules.

i)   Join the circuit on the cross-wind leg close to the airfield boundary and complete the landing in the usual way.

18   *j*)   Report arrival to airfield control.

Action to be Taken when Lost

a)   Log the time 'Lost Procedure' is commenced.

b)   Check the fuel and decide if there is sufficient to continue flying: if not prepare for a forced landing with power.

c)   Check the DI and if it differs with the correct heading ascertain the direction and the amount of error, thus indicating the locality of the Tr. Req. in relation to the aeroplane. Compare the DI with the compass and make sure it is functioning correctly.

d)   Throughout these checks maintain the pre-determined heading.

e)   If Compass Heading and DI are correct and the position of the aircraft in relation to track is unknown adopt one of the following methods.

1. Circle of Uncertainty

a)   Estimate the present DR position had the flight continued as planned, either with reference to the time marks or by calculating the distance flown since the last certain pinpoint.

b)   Using the DR position as a centre draw a circle with a radius which is roughly one-tenth of the distance flown since the last known position. The aircraft is likely to be within that area.

c)   Look for any prominent features within the circle of uncertainty and attempt to find them on the ground. Log any major pinpoints seen. Continue reading from ground to map and endeavour to build up a sequence of features which will fit within the circle of uncertainty.

d)   Proceed until a feature is recognized without doubt, when it will be possible to estimate a heading to destination, or failing this until an airfield appears.

2. Line Feature Method

a)   Study the map on either side of Track and ahead of the farthest possible position of the aircraft. Endeavour to find a good line feature – a river, canal or main railway line will do provided it extends for some distance.

b)   Alter heading so that the line feature will be intercepted at approximately 90 ° and continue flying until it appears.

c)   Dependent upon the location of the feature in relation to the destination, turn and follow the line, logging all important pinpoints together with the heading of the aircraft at the time. Build up a chain of features which will eventually fit the map.

d)   Continue until a position is recognized without doubt and estimate   **18** a heading to destination, or failing this until an alternative airfield appears.

THE PHONETIC ALPHABET

A	Alfa	· —	N	November	— ·
B	Bravo	— · · ·	O	Oscar	— — —
C	Charlie	— · — ·	P	Papa	· — — ·
D	Delta	— · ·	Q	Quebec	— — · —
E	Echo	·	R	Romeo	· — ·
F	Foxtrot	· · — ·	S	Sierra	· · ·
G	Golf	— — ·	T	Tango	—
H	Hotel	· · · ·	U	Uniform	· · —
I	India	· ·	V	Victor	· · · —
J	Juliett	· — — —	W	Whisky	· — —
K	Kilo	— · —	X	X-ray	— · · —
L	Lima	· — · ·	Y	Yankee	— · — —
M	Mike	— —	Z	Zulu	— — · ·

19 Instrument Appreciation

The aim of this exercise is to convince the student that before he has become proficient in instrument flying he must on no account fly in weather conditions that preclude the use of outside visual references.

Throughout this book reference has been made to instrument indications, however all the exercises so far described will have been demonstrated by the instructor and practised by the student in VMC. The importance to a pilot of outside visual references will by now be clear yet, in many countries, experience shows that when a Private Pilot's Licence is gained and confidence grows this very fundamental truth of flying is sometimes forgotten. Many are the incidents, recorded and unrecorded, where inexperienced pilots have continued flying into weather conditions that demanded the use of instruments, sometimes with very serious consequences. Often these situations are the result of 'familiarity breeds contempt'; over-confidence born of the mistaken belief that because the aircraft is fitted with a proper flight panel and various radio aids 'I could cope in an emergency'. The purpose of this exercise is to impress upon the student pilot that, without proper tuition and adequate practice, instrument flying is not to be attempted. On no account should it be regarded as a do-it-yourself activity. Equally an acceptable level of instrument flying proficiency is within the reach of all students capable of attaining a Private Pilot's Licence.

So important is instrument flying to the operation of aircraft under modern air traffic conditions that a separate rating must be gained by pilots wishing to fly within certain types of controlled airspace and in IMC. In order of seniority these are –

The Instrument Rating

The Private Pilot's Instrument Rating
The IMC Rating (recognised in the UK only)

A comprehensive chapter on instruments and instrument flying and details of the IMC Rating Course are included in *Flight Briefing for Pilots, Volume 2* Ex. 19 and Chapter 12). *The Instrument Rating* covers the requirements of that qualification. The present chapter is confined to the briefest details and, as already explained, is intent upon impressing the student with the serious consequences of attempting untutored instrument flight in low cloud or poor visibility.

The Instrument Panel

By international agreement the main instruments used for determining an aircraft's performance and attitude are grouped together in a standard presentation known as the **Basic 'T' Flight Panel.** This is illustrated in Fig. 99. Although the various instruments can in themselves differ very considerably in general design and the amount of information presented, the basic 'T' layout is common to all modern civil aircraft irrespective of size.

Function of the Instruments

By now the information provided by the various instruments will be understood by the student pilot. A demonstration was included in the **Straight and Level Flight** exercise (page 56) and in fact reference has been made to the instruments in most of the exercises that comprise the PPL syllabus. However these references were made for the purpose of –

(*a*) familiarizing the student with the instruments
and
(*b*) as a cross check on outside visual references for the purpose of attaining accuracy.

So far no attempt will have been made to fly with sole reference to the instruments and this is quite another matter,

19

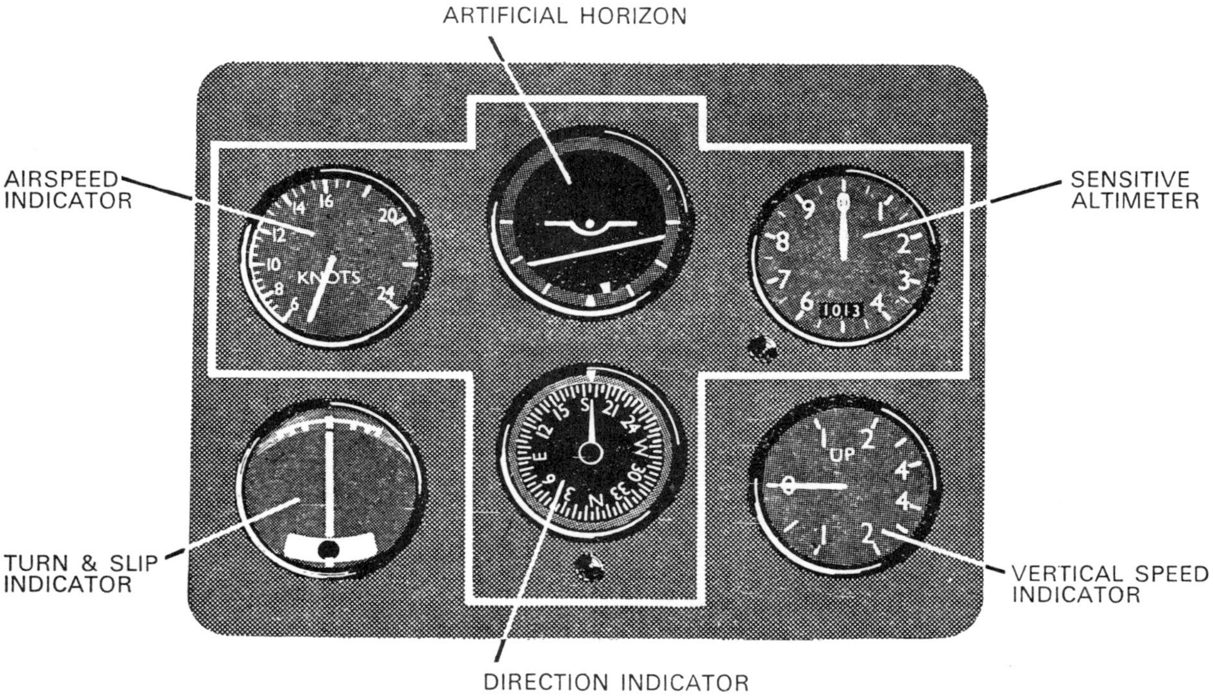

SENSITIVE ALTIMETER

VERTICAL SPEED INDICATOR

ARTIFICIAL HORIZON

DIRECTION INDICATOR

AIRSPEED INDICATOR

TURN & SLIP INDICATOR

Fig. 99. 'Basic T' Flight Panel.

bringing into play skills that are the result of correct instruction and practice under supervision.

Toppling Limits of Instruments

The instruments on the flight panel may be divided into two categories –

1. **Pressure Instruments.** Those which provide their information by sampling static or pressure air (or both) from the pitot head or in some aircraft the pressure head/static vent. The Airspeed Indicator, Altimeter and Vertical Speed Indicator are in this category.

2. **Gyro-operated Instruments.** Those providing attitude and turn information using the properties of rigidity provided by a gyroscope. This may be driven by vacuum, usually from an engine-driven pump, or by electric power. The Artificial Horizon, Direction Indicator and the turn portion of the Turn and Slip Indicator are the gyro-operated instruments.

Because of the mechanical problems inherent in providing a gyro with complete freedom of movement while at the same time ensuring a supply of air to drive it, all early gyro instruments and indeed some modern examples have limiting stops to keep the rotor within its air jets. When some extreme aircraft attitude causes the gyro to come up against its stops some instruments will behave in a manner similar to a child's spinning top in the last stages of slowing down. The resultant movement of the gyro will cause the Artificial Horizon to fluctuate, random fashion, from maximum left bank to maximum right, at the same time indicating violent changes in pitch attitude, while the Direction Indicator will spin intermittently. These indications will continue after the aircraft has regained straight and level flight and while the DI may be re-set with its heading knob an Artificial Horizon will require 10 minutes or more for the automatic corrective device to stabilize the instrument. When, following some extreme flight attitude, gyro instruments behave in the manner described they are said to have **Toppled** and the angular limits where a gyro reaches its

19

stops are known as **Toppling Limits** (expressed in degrees). Although some modern instruments have complete freedom of movement throughout 360° in both the lateral and longitudinal planes many do not and since toppling is the result of allowing an aircraft to attain some unusual attitude an out-of-hand situation could very well result in loss of indications from the Artificial Horizon and the Direction Indicator, a further danger of untutored instrument flying.

While it is not intended at this stage that the student should have a detailed knowledge of instruments it should be noted that the turn-needle gyro has freedom of movement in one plane only. Like the other gyro instruments, it has limiting stops, but when these are reached the gyro does not topple. In other words the Turn-and-Slip Indicator will continue to provide valuable attitude information after the Artificial Horizon has toppled. While this is one of the values of the instrument, interpreting its indications and translating these into control movements calls for a higher level of skill than does instrument flight with the aid of an Artificial Horizon. The task is not one that should be attempted by pilots without previous experience of flying on the **Limited Panel.**

Precision Appreciation

At this stage of the course a student will have used the instruments as an aid to achieving precision flight, e.g. turns at the correct angle of bank (Artificial Horizon), turns at a particular rate (Turn Needle), correct balance (Slip Indicator), correct heading (Direction Indicator) and a particular rate of climb or descent (Vertical Speed Indicator). While this experience is a valuable stepping stone towards instrument flight it must again be emphasized that, in itself, this will not enable a pilot to dispense with outside visual references and control the aircraft by reading the instruments on the flight panel.

Physiological Considerations

Human limitations constitute an important problem of **19**

instrument flying. Such is the nature of our balance mechanism and nervous system that without visual references it is difficult to maintain a required attitude unless full use is made of muscle response. For example with both feet on the ground an upright position may easily be maintained with the eyes closed. Raise one foot off the ground and the task becomes more difficult. Spin around several times with the eyes closed, then try standing on one foot. Most people find this impossible because the balance mechanism has been disturbed.

Likewise in an aircraft a pilot denied outside visual references due to cloud or poor visibility would be unable to hold a required heading or maintain level flight unless he could interpret the instruments before him. And this in itself is only part of the problem. Carry out a series of steep turns in one direction then level out and the nervous system will insist that the aircraft is turning in the opposite direction although it is in straight and level flight. Experienced pilots learn to put their trust in the instruments before them. On the other hand a non-instrument pilot with few flying hours is a natural prey to his own nervous system and the very instincts that may protect him on the ground could well put him at risk in the air.

This chapter and the air exercise that now follows is not intended to frighten, rather it is aimed at instilling at little realism into the minds of those otherwise admirable students of limited experience who, on occasions, may perhaps suffer from a little overconfidence.

Provided the exercise has been demonstrated correctly by the flying instructor and accepted in the correct spirit by the student pilot the end product should be a determination to obtain an instrument qualification at the first opportunity after gaining a Private Pilot's Licence.

Flight Practice

Note. To obtain full value from this exercise the aircraft should be equipped with approved screens or two-stage amber. While instruments hoods are better than nothing at all few of these com-

19

pletely obscure all outside visual references and they should only be used when screens are not available.

The Instructor must not attempt to teach instrument flying in this exercise.

The Instrument Panel

a)   The aircraft is now flying straight and level at a constant height, heading and airspeed. This is confirmed by the instruments.

b)   Note the position of the aircraft symbol which is level with the horizon bar in the Artificial Horizon.

c)   Now take over the controls and maintain the aircraft at its present height and on the existing heading.

Attitude Flight

a)   Ignore the performance instruments and concentrate on holding a level attitude on the Artificial Horizon.

b)   Notice that small angles of bank produce an immediate change in heading. There is a tendency to over control in bank and, to a lesser extent, in pitch.

Physiological Considerations

a)   After holding a steep turn for several moments the aircraft is now being returned to straight and level flight.

b)   Now try flying on instruments. There is a strong tendency to correct a turn that does not exist. The instruments confirm the aircraft to be flying approximately straight and level.

Toppling Limits

(When the instruments are of a type that can be toppled the following should be demonstrated allowing the pupil to see out of the aircraft) –

a)   The aircraft is now flying normally with the instruments functioning correctly.

b)   Imagine that due to mishandling an extreme attitude beyond the limits of some instruments has been attained (usually a steep pull-up followed by a wing over will reproduce the situation without exceeding the limits of the aircraft or upsetting the student under training). **19** *c)*   The Artificial Horizon and the Direction Indicator (according to the type of instrument) have toppled although the turn needle continues to provide useful information.

d)   Re-set the Direction Indicator with the heading knob.

e)   Note the time required for the Artificial Horizon to re-erect and provide normal indications.

Notice to Instructors

While the student attempts to fly the aircraft on instruments deviations from height, heading and airspeed, together with attitude indications, should be drawn to his attention. In allowing him to make his own mistakes a situation must not develop where the aircraft could exceed its V_{ne} or the pupil may become alarmed.

Appendix 1 – Graphs

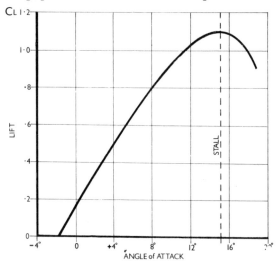

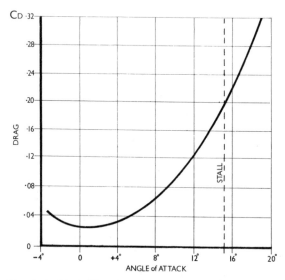

Graph 1. (*Top*) Showing changes in lift at various angles of attack. (*Lower*) Behaviour of drag with changes in angle of attack.

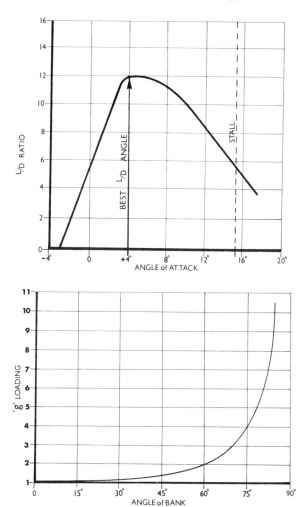

Graph 2. (*Top*) The relationship between angle of attack and lift/drag ratio.

(*Lower*) Loading during turns at various angles of bank.

Note that up to 60° Bank loading is moderate, doubling over the next 15° and reaching 10'g' at 84° Angle of Bank.

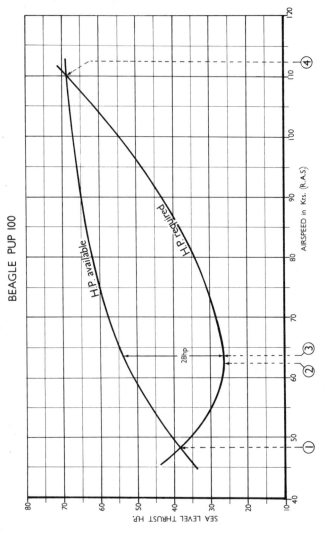

Graph 3. HP available/HP required.

HP Available and HP Required

A considerable amount of interesting information may be derived from these curves, the example shown above relating to the Beagle Pup 100. Before examining the graph these terms of reference should be understood –

1 **Thrust HP (Vertical Scale).** This is engine Brake Horsepower less power lost by the propeller while converting power into thrust.

2 **HP Available (Top Curve).** This curve represents sea level power at full throttle. Since the aircraft used in this example is fitted with a fixed pitch propeller, reductions in airspeed will increase the blade angle of attack, increase the load on the engine so causing a decrease in RPM and of course BHP. As altitude is gained and air density decreases so the HP available curve will descend down the graph.

3 **HP Required (Lower Curve).** In effect this curve could also be labelled 'total drag' because it represents the amount of power needed to balance drag at any particular airspeed.

The following information may now be extracted from the curves –

1 **Propeller Efficiency.** Assuming the engine to produce a net 90 BHP it will be seen that a maximum speed (and power) thrust HP is in the region of 70 THP (i.e. power available for propelling the aircraft) indicating a propeller efficiency of approximately 78 per cent.

2 **Minimum Speed (1).** Note the sharp rise in horsepower required as speed is reduced below 60 kt. This is because of the considerable increase in induced drag which occurs at high angles of attack (page 54). At the low speed power available is at its lowest and where the two curves meet corresponds to Minimum Speed. A further reduction in speed would cause a loss of height.

3 **Maximum Endurance (2).** The speed at which total drag is at its lowest value will likewise be the speed which requires the least power for level flight and in consequence the lowest fuel consumption in gallons (pounds or kilos) per hour. This will not produce maximum range (i.e. best air miles per gallon), speed for maximum range being rather higher than speed for maximum endurance.

4 **Maximum Speed (4).** The HP required curve shows a steady increase as speed is developed above 60 kt thus indicating a similar build up of total drag. When power required reaches the level of power available (position 4) any further increase in speed will cause a descent. In other words maximum level speed is indicated by the point at which the two curves again meet.

5 **Maximum Rate of Climb (3).** In the chapter on Climbing (page 59) it was explained that power surplus to requirements was used to climb the aircraft. At 64 kt (RAS) there is a surplus of rather more than 28 HP over and above that required for level flight at this speed. Remembering that 1 HP is the equivalent of 33,000 lb raised 1 ft in one minute, the surplus 28 HP may be calculated in terms of rate of climb quite simply –

$$\text{Rate of Climb} = \frac{\text{surplus HP} \times 33{,}000}{\text{weight of aircraft (lb)}}$$

$$= \frac{28 \times 33{,}000}{1{,}600} = 577 \text{ ft/min rate of climb}$$

The Pup is unusual in so far as a similar level of surplus horsepower available for climbing is obtainable over a wide range of speeds. Reference to the curves shows that rate of climb will remain fairly constant between 64 kt and 78 kt RAS, steepest climb gradient occurring at the lowest speed within the range (64 kt RAS corresponding on the Beagle Pup to an Indicated Air Speed of 60 kt).

Appendix 2 – Ground Signals

Runway or taxiway unfit for aircraft landing or manoeuvring.

Area to be used only for take-off and landing of helicopters.

Movement of aircraft and gliders confined to hard surface areas.

Direction of take-off and landing may differ. (Also shown by a black ball suspended from the signals mast.)

A red L on the above sign indicates that light aircraft may land on runway or grass area. (May also be used in conjunction with signal below.)

A yellow diagonal on a red square means special care is necessary in landing, owing to temporary obstruction or other reason.

Landing and take-off on runways only, but movement not confined to hard surfaces.

Landing prohibited — a yellow cross on a red square.

Glider flying in progress. (Used in conjunction with two red balls on the signals mast.)

Right hand circuit in force. The arrow is made up of red and yellow stripes.

Shaft of the T indicates direction of take-off or landing — i.e. towards the crossbar.

Part of the manoeuvring area to be used only for the take-off and landing of light aircraft.